DAVID WAUGH

PLACE AND PEOPLE
Comparative Case Studies

Text © David Waugh 2001

Original line illustrations © Nelson Thornes Ltd 2001

The right of David Waugh to be identified as author of this work has been asserted by him in accordance with the Copyright, Designs and Patents Act 1988.

All rights reserved. No part of this publication may be reproduced or transmitted in any form or by any means, electronic or mechanical, including photocopy, recording or any information storage and retrieval system, without permission in writing from the publisher or under licence from the Copyright Licensing Agency Limited. Further details of such licences (for reprographic reproduction) may be obtained from the Copyright Licensing Agency Limited, of 90 Tottenham Court Road, London W1P 0LP.

First published in 2001 by:
Nelson Thornes
Delta Place
27 Bath Road
CHELTENHAM GL53 7TH
England

01 02 03 04 05 / 10 9 8 7 6 5 4 3 2 1

A catalogue record for this book is available from the British Library.

ISBN 0-17-434320-5

Design, layout and illustration by Hardlines Ltd, Charlbury, Oxford
Edited by Katherine James
Picture research by Penni Bickle

Printed and bound in Croatia by Zrinski d. d. Cadovec

Acknowledgements

With thanks to the following for permission to reproduce photographs and other copyright material in this book:

Arcaid fig 4.6; **Associated Press** figs 9.4, 9.5, 9.10, 9.16; **Channel 4** figs 2.7, 4.9, 4.10, 4.11, 4.12, 4.13, 5.1, 5.2, 5.3, 5.4, 5.5, 5.6, 5.7, 5.8, 5.11, 5.12, 5.13, 5.14, 5.15, 5.17, 5.18, 5.19, 5.23, 5.24, 5.25, 5.26, 5.27, 5.28, 5.29, 5.30, 7.7, 7. 9, 7.10, 7.11, 7.12, 9.12, 9.14, 9.15, 9.17, 10.6, 10.11, 12.7, 12.8, 12.9, 12.10, 12.11, 12.12, 12.14, 12.15, 12.16 (a, b), 12.17, 12.18, 12.19, 12.20, 12.29, 12.31, 12.33; **China Pictorial Publications** figs 12.21, 12.23, 12.24; **Civil Engineering Dept, Hong Kong** 9.23; **Daily Telegraph/David Burgess** fig 10.4; **Eye Ubiquitous** figs 2.6, 4.2; **Impact** fig 4.27; **Katherine James** figs 3.4a&b; **David Money** figs 2.19, 6.3, 6.4, 6.13, 6.18, 6.19, 6.20, 6.21, 6.22, 6.23, 7.1, 12.25, 12.26; **News Team International/Sharp/Greenwood** fig 10.3; **Peter Pedley** figs 3.6, 3.8; **Rex Features** fig 11.5; **Dick Roberts** figs 11.11, 11.12; **Chris Rowley** figs 2.10, 2.13, 2.14, 2.15, 2.16, 2.18, 3.11, 3.12, 3.13, 3.14, 3.15, 3.16, 3.17, 3.18, 3.19, 3.20, 3.21, 4.14, 4.15, 4.16, 4.21, 4.22, 4.23, 4.24, 4.25, 5.21, 5.22, 6.2, 6.5, 6.8, 6.9, 6.11, 6.12, 6.14, 6.24, 6.25, 6.26, 6.27, 6.30, 6.31, 6.33, 7.3, 7.4, 7.5, 7.6, 7.14 a&b, 7.15, 7.16, 7.17, 7.18, 7.19, 7.20, 7.22, 7.23, 7.24, 7.25, 7.28, 8.5, 8.6, 8.7, 8.8, 9.19, 10.13, 10.14, 10.15, 10.16, 12.28, 12.32, 12.39; **Still Pictures** figs 4.1, 9.1, 10.8, 11.6, 11.7, 12.3; **David Waugh** figs 2.12, 2.20, 3.23, 3.24, 4.17, 4.18, 4.19, 4.20, 6.6, 6.7, 6.10, 6.15, 6.16, 6.17, 6.28, 6.29, 6.32, 7.21, 7.29, 8.9, 8.10, 9.9, 9.21, 10.12, 12.22, 12.30, 12.37, 12.38, 12.34, 12.40.

Every effort has been made to contact copyright holders. The publishers apologise to anyone whose rights have been inadvertently overlooked, and will be happy to rectify any errors or omissions.

This book has been produced by Nelson Thornes in collaboration with 4Learning, the educational division of Channel 4 Television. It has been written to link with programmes from the Channel 4 schools series *Place and People*, for 14–16 year-olds, and *Geographical Eye* (12–14 year-olds). In particular, the book has links with programmes from the following units:

Place and People: Changing China
Place and People: Italy
Geographical Eye over Britain (1)
Geographical Eye over Asia

The matrix on pages 94–95 shows the links between chapters in the book and specific programmes in these series. All the programmes have been screened by Channel 4, and are available on video from 4Learning. Details of how to purchase these videos are given on page 95.

Contents

1. Physical contrasts in China — 4
2. Population changes — 8
3. Changing villages — 16
4. Urban management — 24
5. Farming and industry in Italy and India — 34
6. Farming in China — 42
7. Industry in China — 50
8. Changes in energy — 58
9. Hazards — 62
10. River flooding and management — 70
11. Climatic issues — 76
12. Environmental concerns — 82

Multimedia cross-reference matrix — 94

Index — 96

Photographs with this symbol are still images taken from the Channel 4 schools television series *Place and People* and *Geographical Eye*.

Physical contrasts in China

Climatic contrasts

China is, by area, the fourth largest country in the world (1.1). It extends from 18°N (the same latitude as Jamaica) to 53°N (similar to that of Manchester) and from 73°E to 134°E (i.e. about one-sixth of the way around the globe). Given the size of China, it is hardly surprising that there is a wide range of climatic types and physical regions within the country.

Factors affecting climate

1 Prevailing winds Prevailing winds bring warm weather if they pass over warm surfaces (the land in summer or the sea in winter), and cold weather if they blow over cold surfaces (the land in winter or the sea in summer). They also bring wet weather when they blow from the sea and dry weather when they come from the land.

China's climate is dominated by the seasonal reversal of the direction of the prevailing wind, an event referred to as the monsoon (the term 'monsoon' means season). From November to April pressure is high over Central Asia. The high pressure creates outblowing winds which, because central Asia is cold and dry at this time of year, are cold and dry (the winter monsoon – 1.2a). In contrast, pressure is low over Central Asia between May and October. The low pressure leads to inblowing winds which, because they originate in the tropics and blow across large sea areas, are warm and wet (the summer monsoon – 1.2b).

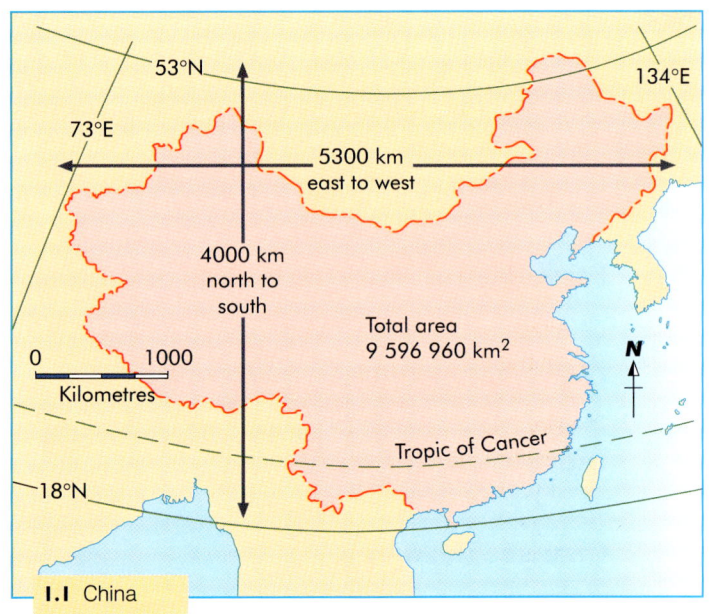

1.1 China

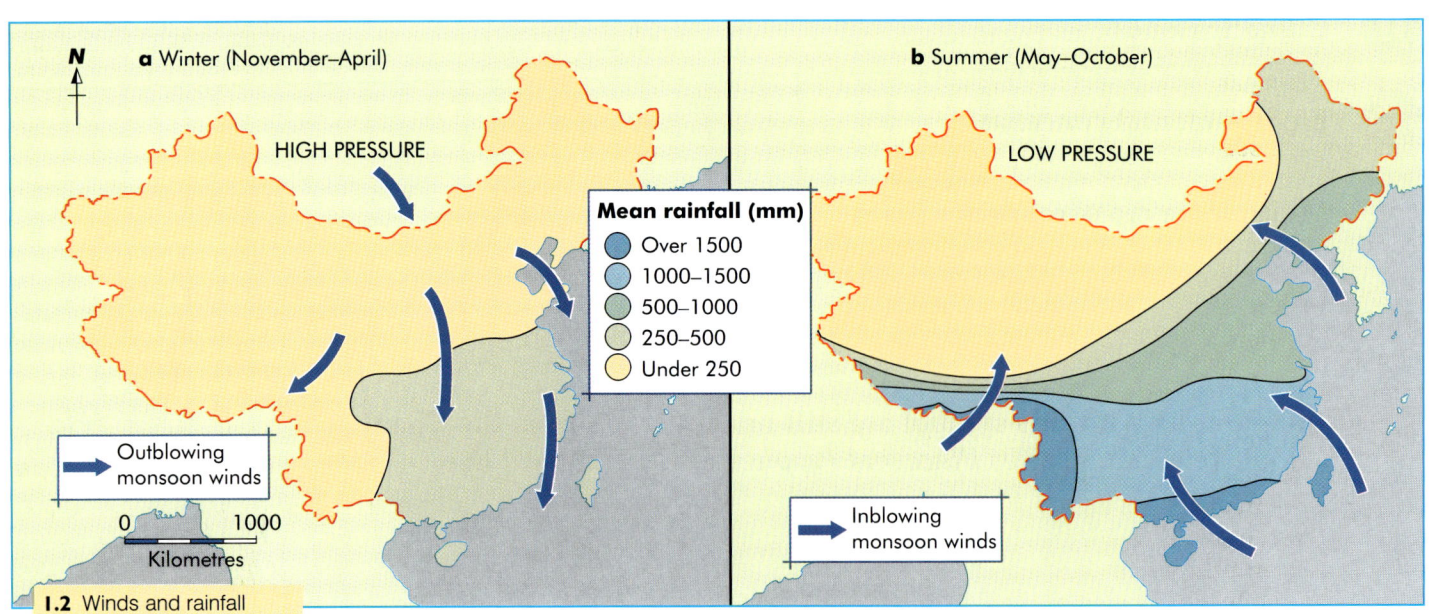

1.2 Winds and rainfall

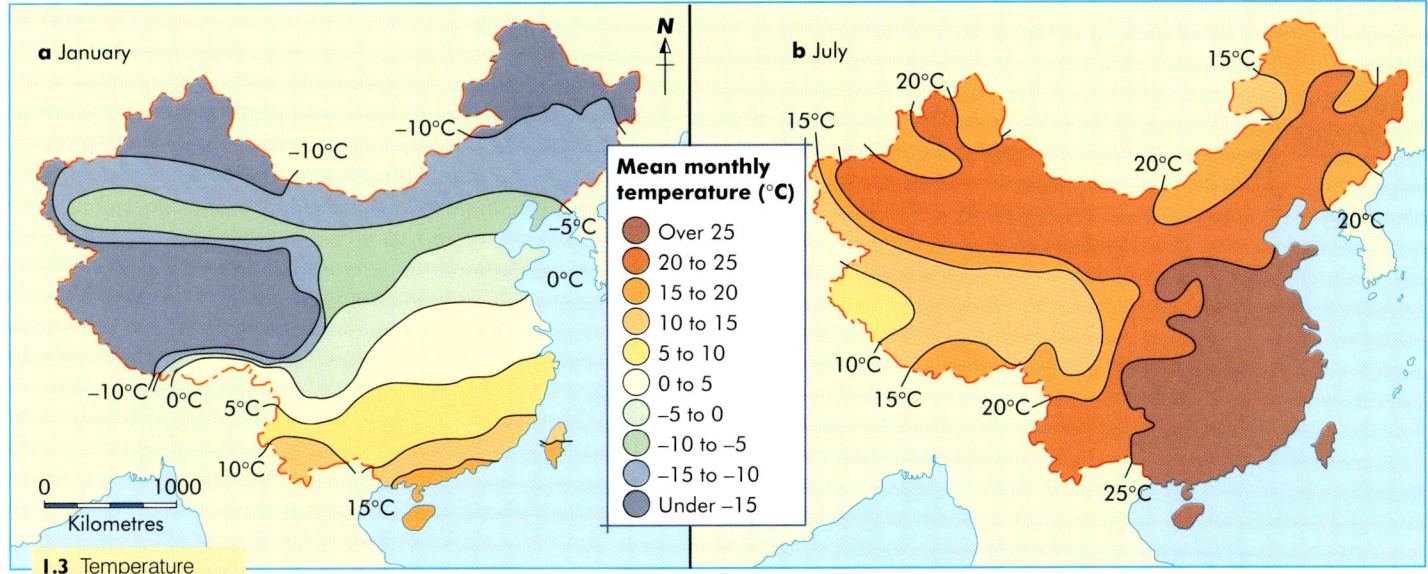

1.3 Temperature

2 Latitude Places near to the Equator are much warm than places nearer the poles. This is due to the curvature of the Earth and the angle of the sun in the sky. Where the sun is high in the sky it concentrates its heat upon a much smaller area, and therefore warms it more rapidly, than where it is low in the sky. Also, the steeper the sun's angle, the more rapidly its rays pass through the atmosphere. This means that less heat is lost to gases, dust and cloud.

As southern parts of China lie within the tropics, their temperatures remain high throughout the year. Although temperatures of places in the north of the country remain high during summer (**1.3a**), they are often very low during winter when the sun's angle in the sky is much lower (**1.3b**).

3 Distance from the sea As the sea (a liquid) can be heated to a much greater depth than the land (a solid), it takes longer to heat up than the land in summer. Once warmed, however, the sea retains its heat much longer in winter and so cools down less quickly than the land. This means that places near the coast have cooler summers, warmer winters and a smaller annual range of temperature (a maritime climate) than places that are inland (a continental climate). Coastal areas are also likely to receive more rainfall, especially when winds blow from the sea, than places that are a long way inland.

Because of the moderating influence of the sea, places in eastern China have a much lower annual range of temperature than continental areas in the west. They also receive much more rainfall than places inland, especially in summer when the rain-bearing monsoon winds blow from the sea (**1.2b**). Inland areas of western China tend to have hot summers, very cold winters and limited annual amounts of rainfall.

4 Altitude (relief) Temperatures decrease, on average, by 1°C for every 100 metres in height. In China, temperatures decrease westwards where the height of the land increases to well over 4000 metres on the Plateau of Tibet (**1.3** and **1.6**).

The monsoon climate

Winter monsoon (November to May) During winter, when the overhead sun is in the southern hemisphere, temperatures fall rapidly over Central Asia and north-western China. This creates a large area of high pressure which, in turn, produces outblowing winds. As these continental regions are dry and cold at this time of year, then so too are the prevailing outblowing winds. The strong winds frequently carry dust eastwards from inland deserts and the loess plateau (see **1.6**). Winters become milder towards the south-east of the country as the angle of the sun in the sky becomes higher (latitude) and the moderating influence of the sea increases, and in sheltered basins such as Sichuan (between Chengdu and Chongqing).

Summer monsoon (June to October) As the overhead sun appears to move northwards (it is overhead at noon in Hong Kong in June), temperatures over Central Asia and north-western China rise rapidly. The high temperatures cause warm air to rise, creating an area of low pressure which in turn results in inblowing winds. As these prevailing winds blow from tropical areas and often have to cross large expanses of sea, they are warm and become very moist. Most of southern and eastern China becomes hot, humid and wet. The monsoon rain is heavy, although by no means continuous, and is often associated with tropical storms that are frequent at this time of year. These tropical storms, known in South-east Asia as typhoons, with their torrential rainfall and severe winds, can be a major climatic hazard. In contrast, western China remains relatively dry, as the winds have shed most of their moisture before reaching here.

Climate and physical regions

Climatic regions

Figure 1.4 shows the variation of climatic types in China. You should remember, however, that as this map covers a large area of land, then:

- it is very generalised and does not show local variations in climate
- it shows borders between climatic types as a line, whereas in reality there are often broad transition zones where different climatic types merge
- it shows average conditions taken over a period of time and does not show small-scale fluctuations such as a year of drought or exceptionally high temperatures.

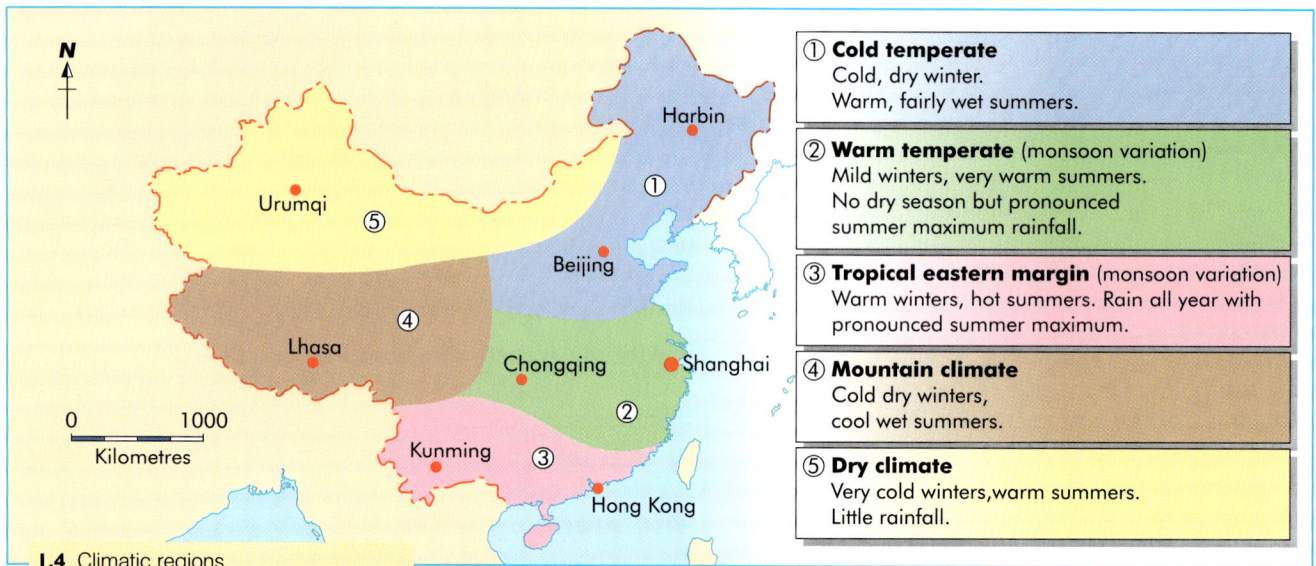

1.4 Climatic regions

① **Cold temperate**
Cold, dry winter. Warm, fairly wet summers.

② **Warm temperate** (monsoon variation)
Mild winters, very warm summers. No dry season but pronounced summer maximum rainfall.

③ **Tropical eastern margin** (monsoon variation)
Warm winters, hot summers. Rain all year with pronounced summer maximum.

④ **Mountain climate**
Cold dry winters, cool wet summers.

⑤ **Dry climate**
Very cold winters, warm summers. Little rainfall.

		Temperature °C			Precipitation		
		Jan	July	Range	% May–Oct	% Nov–April	Annual total (mm)
①	Harbin	−20	23	43	12	88	577
	Beijing	−5	26	31	8	92	619
②	Shanghai	4	28	24	33	67	1138
	Chongqing	7	29	22	22	78	1088
③	Hong Kong	16	29	13	17	83	2169
	Kunming	14	24	10	16	84	967
④	Lhasa	−2	16	18	7	93	408
⑤	Urumqi	−17	14	31	43	57	292

1.5 Climatic data for selected places

1 North-eastern China Winters are very cold, increased by a high wind-chill, with frequent light snowfalls and lengthy periods of frost. Rivers to the north of Harbin may be frozen for four to six months and snow may lie for up to 150 days each year. Further south, around Beijing, strong outblowing winds can cause dust storms. Summers are warm and humid and although rainfall may be sufficient for cultivation, it tends to be unreliable and drought occurs in some years.

2 Central eastern China Winters are not unlike those in western Europe, with the climate alternating between periods of mild and wet weather and spells of colder, drier weather with frost and a little snow (up to 10 days a year in Shanghai). However, summers are much warmer than in western Europe and are very humid. Summer is also the wettest time of year due to the inblowing monsoon winds which bring warm, moist air from the Pacific Ocean and the China Sea. Amounts are higher in coastal areas due to the increase in frequency of typhoons (tropical cyclones). Farther inland, especially in the sheltered Sichuan Basin, winters are milder and summers drier than in places nearer the coast.

3 Southern China The south-east, part of which lies within the tropics, is the warmest and wettest part of China. Winters are very mild, frost and snow are virtually unknown, and it is relatively dry. Summers are very warm and extremely humid (at times the weather can be oppressive). The inblowing warm, moisture-laden monsoon winds, together with frequent typhoons and their violent winds and heavy downpours, make this the wettest time of the year. Further west, in Yunnan, the climate is affected by an increase in altitude. Winters are sunny, relatively dry, and temperatures are mild to warm (Yunnan is known as 'The land of eternal spring'). Summers are pleasantly warm and wet, although some sheltered valleys can be quite dry.

4 South-western China This region consists of high mountains enclosing the Plateau of Tibet. Winters are extremely long and cold, with frequent light snow, hard frosts and a high wind-chill. Although daytime temperatures can be quite high during the summer, they drop rapidly at night. Summer is also the wettest time of the year due to inblowing monsoon winds. Throughout the year the air is clear and sunshine totals are high.

5 North-western China This region has a continental climate, due to its distance from the sea. Winters are long and cold (snow can lie for well over 100 days a year) and dust storms, generated by strong winds, are a common hazard. In contrast, summers are short, humidity is low, and it can be very warm. Although rainfall is fairly evenly distributed throughout the year, amounts are low and decrease westwards from the steppes of Inner Mongolia to the semi-desert and desert regions of the extreme north-west.

Physical regions

As with climate, it is difficult to divide China into broad physical regions. The simplest grouping suggests that the land falls from west to east in three main 'terraces' (**1.6**).

A The western terrace includes the Plateau of Tibet, averaging between 4000 and 5000 m, which is bordered by fold mountains that include, to the south, the Himalayas and the recently re-surveyed Mt Everest rising to 8850 m.
B The middle terrace, mainly between 1000 and 2000 m, includes the dissected Yunnan Plateau and the easily eroded loess plateau of Shaanxi.
C The lower terrace, mainly under 200 m, includes the coastal plain and the lower basins of China's two main rivers, the Huang He and the Yangtze.

China's rivers, responding to the country's relief, flow in a general west-to-east direction.

1.6 Physical regions

2 Population changes

World trends

The United Nations Population Division claimed that, in October 1999, the world's population reached 6 billion (**2.1**). However, this claim needs to be treated with some caution as at best it can only be an approximation. This is because, for example, census data for most countries is only collected every ten years, many people are unlikely either to return forms or to complete them accurately, and groups of people like refugees or some shanty town dwellers are likely to be excluded or missed. What the claim does show, however, is that the world's population is still growing at 140 persons per minute, which is 78 million more people each year.

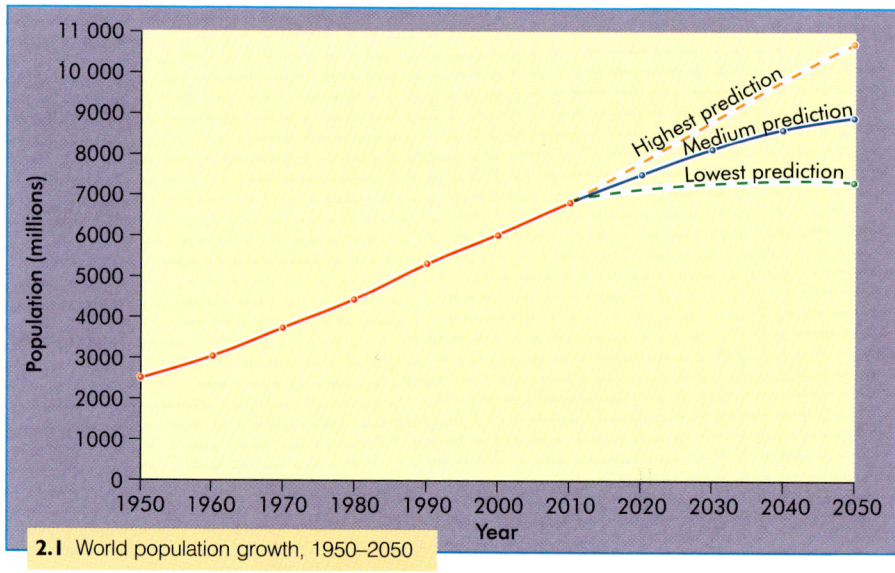

2.1 World population growth, 1950–2050

Recent evidence suggests that even though most people now live longer, the annual rate of population growth is slowing down. This is mainly due to a fall both in the birth rate and in family size (the fertility rate), improvements in family planning and female education, the one-child policy in China (pages 12–13) and, in southern Africa, the effects of AIDS.

The UN predicts that the present annual growth rate of 1.3 per cent (it was 2.1 per cent at its peak in 1970) will drop to 1.0 per cent in 2015 and 0.5 per cent by 2050. This will mean that by the mid-21st century, the world's population will be 8900 million – well below the 11 million predicted in the mid-1970s.

Total fertility rates (TFR)

The total fertility rate (TFR) is one of the best indicators of future population growth (or decline). The TFR is the number of children a woman is expected to have during her lifetime, based on present birth rates. The present world average is just under 3.0. In most economically developed countries the TFR is low and still declining, e.g. UK 1.7 (**2.2**), Japan 1.4 and Italy 1.2. It is, in contrast, much higher in economically less developed countries e.g. Kenya 6.0, India 4.0 and Bangladesh 3.7. Although high birth and fertility rates have long been perceived as a characteristic of 'underdevelopment', the UN now claims that 'a high birth rate is a consequence, not a cause, of poverty' and that, in economically developing countries, one in four births is unwanted by the mother.

BRITAIN'S birth rate has fallen to its lowest level since records began 150 years ago, turning us into a nation of families with 1.7 children.

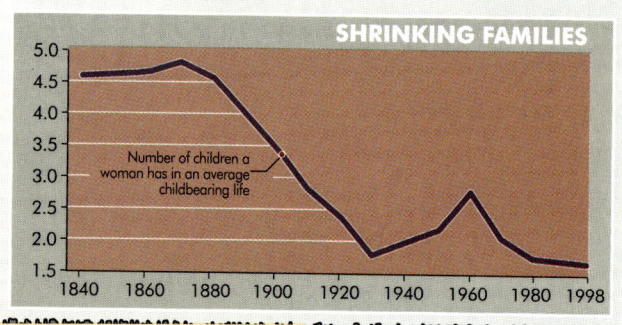

Official statistics reveal that the biggest decline has been among the working class, where the number of families with more than three children has dropped by a third in the past 10 years.

By contrast, experts say the middle classes – caricatured as the suburban family of the early 1970s with 2.3 children and an estate car – has fractured, with increasing numbers spurning children altogether for the sake of their careers or, if they have children, having more.

Britain's population is still rising as more people live longer. On current trends, however, it is expected to start to decline between 2025 and 2050, when the death rate will be higher than the birth rate.

Sunday Times, 25 October 1998

2.2 Britain's declining fertility rate

It is now recognised that the three key factors affecting fertility decline are improvements in the following:

1 Family planning, by
   – increasing the knowledge of contraception methods and access to family planning services
   – reducing the cost, and increasing the supply of, contraception commodities
   – overcoming the disapproval of husbands and family members and the opposition by certain religious groups.

2 Healthcare, including safer abortions and a reduction in infant mortality (the latter means fewer children need to be born as more of them will survive).

3 Women's education, which increases their social status and delays the age of marriage.

However, there are problems in those economically developed countries, and in China with its one-child policy, where the TFR has fallen too low to replace its population. The replacement rate is when there are just sufficient children born to balance the number of people who die. Countries where the replacement rate is not being met face a decrease in population, e.g. Italy from 57 million in 1998 to 41 million by 2050 (**2.3**). They fear that, in time, they will:
- have too few consumers and skilled workers to keep their economy going
- see a reduction in their competitive advantage in science and technology
- experience problems in providing pensions and social care for an ageing population.

	Population (millions)	
	1998	**2050 (est.)**
Germany	82.1	73.3
Italy	57.4	41.2
Japan	126.3	104.9
Spain	39.6	30.2
UK	58.6	56.7

2.3 Declining populations

Increased life expectancy and an ageing population

There has been, initially in the economically more developed countries but also more recently in the economically less developed countries, an increase in life expectancy (**2.4**). By 2000, several countries had over 16 per cent of their population aged over 65 with, for the first time in their history, more people aged over 65 than children aged under 15. In Japan and in parts of western Europe (with the most rapid increases being in Spain and Italy), the proportion of people aged over 65 is expected to reach 35 per cent by 2050. The consequences are likely to be a greater demand for services such as pensions, medical care and residential homes, which will have to be paid for by a smaller percentage of people of working age.

The 1998 official UN population estimates included, for the first time, predictions for the 'oldest-old' – that is, those who are 80 years or older. In 1998, 66 million persons fell into this category, i.e. 1.1 per cent of the world's total population. This number is expected to increase almost six-fold by 2050 to reach 370 million – 311 million being octogenarians (aged 80–89), 57 million being nonagenarians (90–99) and 2 million centenarians (aged over 100).

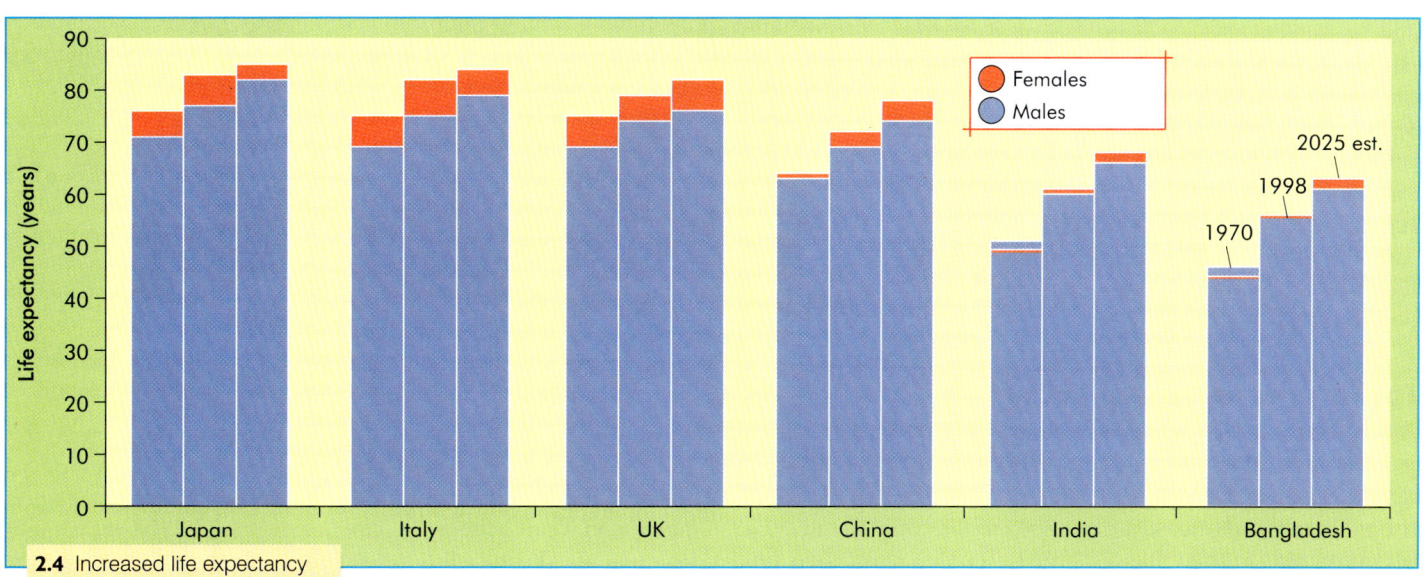

2.4 Increased life expectancy

Italy – changing population structures

Falling fertility rates

Traditionally, Italy has had one of the highest fertility rates in the more economically developed world. This is because it is the centre of the Roman Catholic faith, in which large families are encouraged and contraception and abortion not accepted. Recent attitudes have, however, changed and by the end of the 20th century, Italy's fertility rate was only 1.2 – one of the four lowest in the world.

Fertility rates have fallen most rapidly in recent years in southern Italy (**2.5**). This is because:
- women are more reluctant to fulfil the traditional mother/ housewife role
- more women are working and so, as they become increasingly independent (**5.14**), men are less needed as 'money earners'
- as the infant mortality rate has fallen and the country's standard of living has risen, fewer children are needed for family security
- more men seem to be content to remain bachelors
- jobs are still in short supply, so many young couples delay starting a family
- there has been a recent decline in the Vatican's influence on the country's way of life; contraception is more widely available and attitudes to abortion have become more liberal (although few children are born outside of marriage).

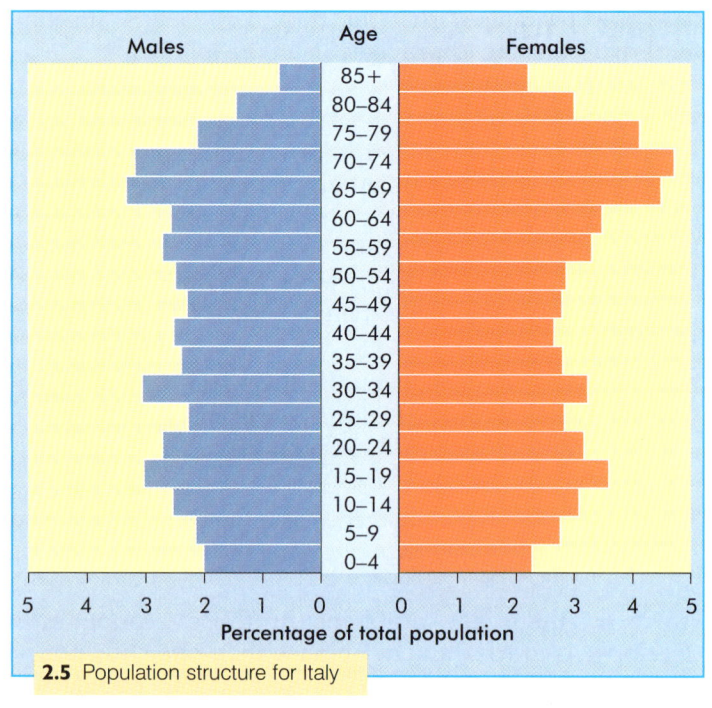

2.5 Population structure for Italy

Increase in life expectancy

Life expectancy in Italy has increased to 79 years for men and 84 for women (**2.4**). At present, 18 per cent of the total population is aged over 65 (**2.5**), a proportion predicted to rise to 35 per cent by 2050. Already the ratio of workers to pensioners is 0.7 (it is 3.5 in the UK), which means that every worker has to support his/her own family and one pensioner. In 2000, 19 per cent of Italy's GNP was spent on looking after the over-65s. Estimates suggest that by 2030 this figure will have risen to an unsustainable 33 per cent (**2.6**).

2.6 Italy's ageing population

Falling replacement rate

As an example, one village in southern Italy had 15 deaths in 1999 and only 3 births, which means that the replacement rate was not met. Between 1970 and 1999, the population of the village had decreased from 3000 to 800, and the number of 8-year-olds in the village school had fallen from 26 in 1990 to 12. The local mayor was threatening to tax those who did not marry and have children, while the state government was talking about raising the pension age and encouraging people to work longer (in Italy, as in the UK, the retirement age was fixed when life expectancy was much shorter).

India – family planning

India's population grew from 358 million in 1950 to 1000 million in 2000 – an average annual growth rate of 12.84 million. If this growth rate continues, India's present population will double by 2035. By then it may well have overtaken China to become the world's most populous country. This is because India's attempts to implement family planning have, so far, failed to reduce significantly its fertility rate (page 8), especially in contrast to China with its more draconian 'one-child' policy (page 12). In 1999, India's fertility rate was 4.0 (**2.7**) and the proportion (percentage) of the total population aged 0–14 was 34 (**2.8**) (the respective figures for China were 1.3 and 25).

2.7 India's young population

As long ago as the early 20th century, India identified that rapid population growth was an obstacle to economic development. Yet it was not until the 1960s that the state created a Family Planning Department aimed at population control. The department stated its desire to see the fertility rate, then at over 6, reduced to 2 by the year 2000. The National Population Policy of 1976 encouraged people to accept compulsory sterilisation, for which they received a payment worth less than £3. However, successive governments were reluctant to tackle the problem of family planning, which they perceived as a vote loser. Figure **2.9** gives the result of a survey on sterilisation methods used by women in the state of Karnataka in the early 1990s.

The United Nations state that there are two basic needs which must be accepted if birth and fertility rates are to be reduced:

1 Improving the status of women and allowing them the right to decide between having more children or birth control.

2 Providing better education, especially for women, on family planning.

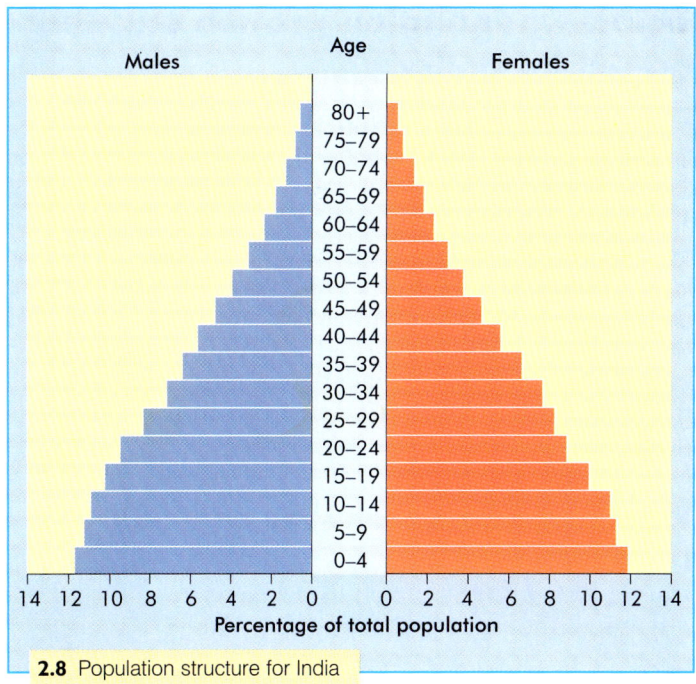

2.8 Population structure for India

In India, local social workers confirm that the most successful method of contraception is not sterilisation, the pill or condoms (**2.9**), but female literacy. They point out that couples living in high-literacy states, especially where girls have had a full-time education, tend to have, on average, only two children. In the more populous states, where fewer people can read, families still often have five or more children.

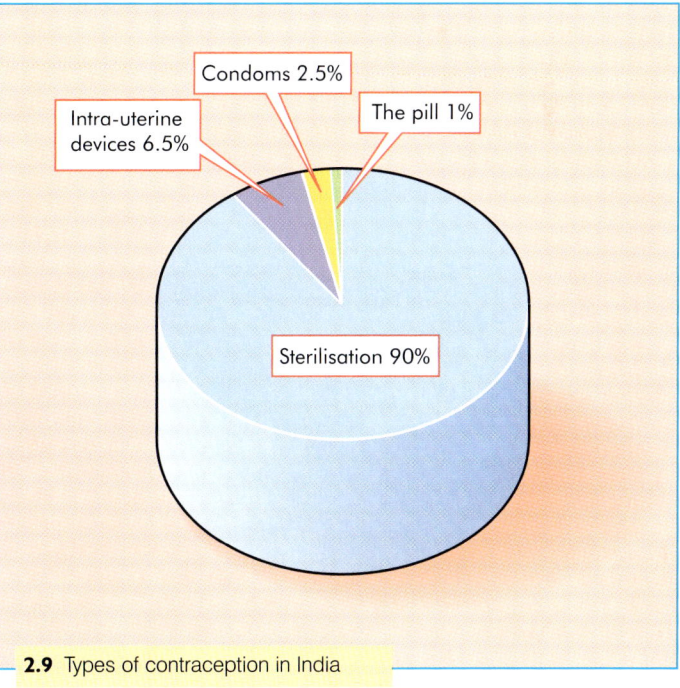

2.9 Types of contraception in India

11

China – population growth and the one-child policy

Distribution and density

China's population of 1.25 billion in 1999 was 21 per cent of the world's total (**2.10**). This gave a population density of 134 per km^2 (compared with 247 in the UK). China's population is not, however, spread evenly across the country, as 94 per cent live on only 40 per cent of the land area – mainly in coastal provinces and the middle and lower Yangtze Basin (**2.11**). This leaves only 6 per cent living in the remaining 60 per cent of the country, coinciding with the more mountainous and desert provinces lying to the north and west.

Population growth and the one-child policy

During the mid-20th century, the Chinese, in response to the state's philosophy that 'a large population gives a strong nation', were encouraged to have as many children as possible. The result was a population growth of 55 million (about the same as the UK's total population) every three years. Concern over this growth rate grew during the 1970s, despite a fall in the birth rate from 44 per 1000 in 1950 to 31 per 1000 in 1975 and in family size from 5 children per family to 3 during the same period. It was suggested that China's optimum, or ideal, population total was 700 million (at the time it was already approaching 100 million), and that an attempt should be made to reduce the country's population to that figure by the year 2080. To achieve this, the average family size (i.e. the total fertility rate) would have to be limited to 1.5 children. The state decided, in 1979, to play safe and to 'forcibly' restrict the size to 1.0 – the 'one-child per family policy' (**2.12**).

At the same time, the marriageable age was set at 22 for men and 20 for women. Couples had to apply to be married and again before having a child. Those who conformed were given free education, priority housing, pensions, and family benefits. Those who did not were deprived of these benefits and were fined heavily – up to 15 per cent of their total income. In an early attempt to enforce the policy, women who became pregnant for a second time were forced to have an abortion, persistent offenders were 'offered' sterilisation, and contraceptive advice was offered to women. The policy was so successful that, since 1987, there has been increasing relaxation of the policy (although human rights activists claim that there were forced abortions and female infanticide as a result of the policy).

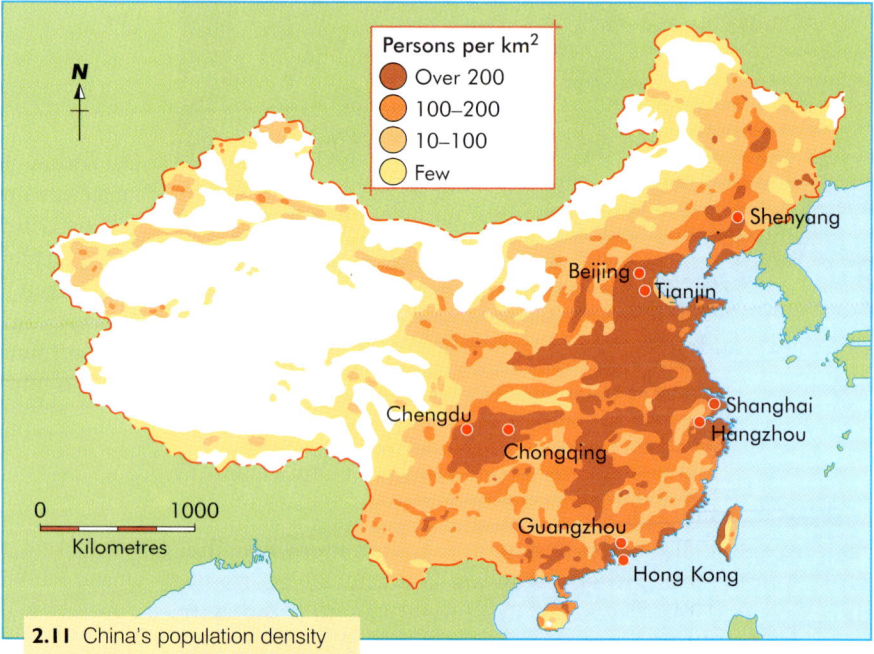

2.11 China's population density

2.10 China has a large population: people in Chengdu

2.12 A one-child family in Kunming, Yunnan

In reality, the one-child policy was more complicated than it appeared. The policy was aimed mainly at the Han majority group, who account for 92 per cent of China's population, rather than the 8 per cent belonging to the remaining 56 other ethnic minority groups. Exceptions included the following groups:

- The Han could apply for a second child if the first was mentally or physically handicapped, or died.
- In many rural areas, farmers could have a second child if the first-born happened to be a girl (although girls did a large proportion of the farmwork, they were considered to be less useful for working in the fields). If the second child was also a girl, then hard luck!
- Han people living in some rural areas could have a second child on payment of a large fine imposed by individual provinces (**2.13**).
- Minority groups, most of whom live in outlying provinces such as Yunnan, were allowed two children (**2.14**) or, if the area was very remote (with fewer officials to keep a check) up to four.
- As the first single-family children are now reaching marriageable age, if two 'only-children' marry then they can have two children.
- In the event of twins, the state paid the extra costs.

Most people, especially those in urban areas, appear to accept the necessity of the policy. Those in their early twenties – the first 'only-children' generation – sometimes admit that they would have liked to have had a brother or sister, but acknowledge that the policy has helped raise their standard of living and given them greater opportunities.

In 1999 the state claimed that China's population was 300 million less than it would have been had the one-child policy not been introduced. Feeling confident that population growth was under control, the authorities in Beijing announced further reductions in birth control restrictions by:
- abolishing quotas for child births in 300 trial districts and replacing them with voluntary family planning education programmes (parents will still have to apply in advance to have a child)
- allowing, for the first time, an informed choice between different kinds of contraception – previously the state said 'we provide this kind of contraception and you must use it' (of contraceptive methods used in 1999, 49 per cent were sterilisation, 44 per cent were intra-uterine devices (IUD), 4 per cent condoms, 2 per cent the pill, and 1 per cent others)
- allowing all families in rural areas to have two children.

2.13 Two brothers and their cousin, in Sichuan

2.14 A Naxi farming family near Lijiang, Yunnan

China – an ageing population and minority ethnic groups

The family, which was central to Confucian society as long ago as the 3rd century BC, remains important in many parts of China (2.15). Grandparents have usually lived with their children and grandchildren. Indeed, more recently, it has been a grandparents' task to look after their grandchildren while the children's parents are out at work.

An ageing population

At present, China is more concerned with its ageing population than it is with its population growth and its number of children (2.16). China's ageing population results from an increase in life expectancy. Life expectancy has increased from 39 for men and 42 for women in 1950, to 69 and 72 respectively in 2000 (2.4) – in other words, a person born in 2000 can expect to live 30 years longer than someone born in 1950. Predictions suggest that the proportion of Chinese aged 60 and over will increase from the 10 per cent of 1998 to 22 per cent by 2030. This change will, according to the *China Business Handbook* (1999), have a massive impact on Chinese society and require urgent reform of the provision of pensions (there are none at present for the majority of the population), healthcare and other benefits. This increase in life expectancy, together with the decline in the fertility rate, has led to significant changes in China's population structure (2.17).

2.16 Ageing Naxi women, Lijiang, Yunnan

There are also signs, especially in large urban areas, of the beginnings of a breakdown in the traditional family way of life. This is because an increasing number of younger, more career-minded couples now prefer to live on their own rather than with their parents. This means that more and more elderly Chinese are being forced to live on their own and will, presumably, have to rely on the state, rather than their children, to support them. In time, more single children are likely to have to support up to two parents and four longer-living grandparents: the so-called 4–2–1 pattern.

The imbalance between the sexes, resulting from the traditional preference for boys, is another concern. Statistics are hard to come by because this is a sensitive subject, but a 1966 government survey revealed that there were 118 newborn boys reported for every 100 girls (the world average was 105 to 100).

2.15 Extreme age groups in a farming village near Xi'an (note the house cut into the loess cliff)

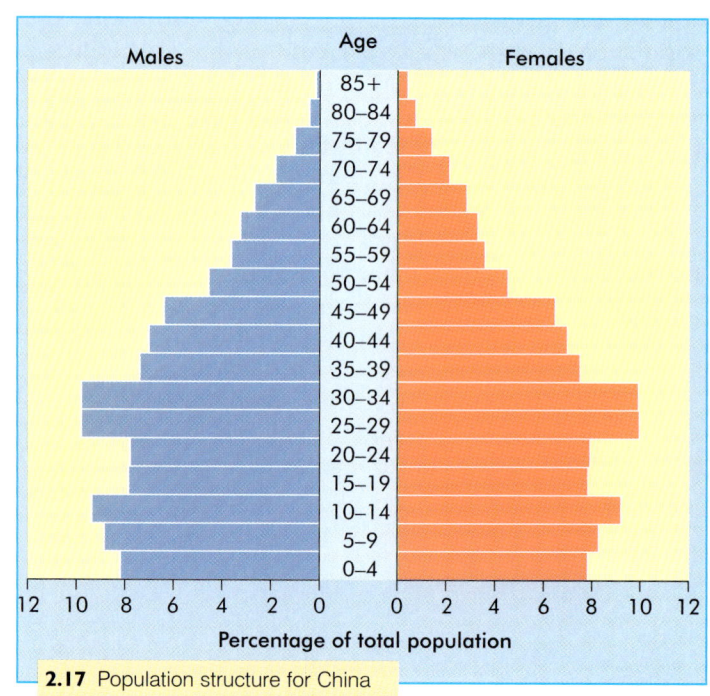

2.17 Population structure for China

14

Madam Li (**2.18**) is 70 and she lives, as she has done since she was married 50 years ago, in an older part of Beijing. Since her husband died she has had to live alone, as her son and daughter, like most younger people, prefer living in modern high-rise apartments. She says that she would hate to have to move from an area where she has lived all her life and where she knows everybody, to the flats where her son lives – he admits that, even after two years of living there, he has yet to speak to any of his neighbours.

The state now accepts that in the not too distant future it will have to look after an increasing number of people like Madam Li who live alone.

Minority ethnic groups

The majority of the Chinese population is ethnic Han. The Han people have their own language, which is also the Chinese language. Although non-Han groups account for only 8 per cent of China's population (page 13), in total they number 108 million. Of the 56 recognised minority ethnic groups, most live near to the country's sparsely populated borders, especially those in the extreme north-west or in Yunnan in the south-west (**2.19**). Of these, 53 use their own spoken language and 23 their own written language. Except in respect of the Tibetans, the Chinese state appears to be relatively tolerant of ethnic minorities, who are allowed to preserve their language, religion and culture and were exempt from the one-child policy. Such concessions are seen, in the eyes of the Han Chinese, as a sign of goodwill.

The Naxi, who live in northern Yunnan, are descended from Tibetan nomads. They have their own written language which is based on pictographs. This, together with their own special music which is played upon ancient instruments, is over 1000 years old. Their religion, called *dongba*, resembles the nature worship of pre-Buddhist Tibet. Naxi women, especially in their main city of Lijiang, appear to do most of the work (although men retain ownership of property). The women (**2.16** and **2.20**) wear blue (representing heaven) blouses and trousers covered by an apron, and a blue cap. The top of the apron is usually black (it may be blue) and the

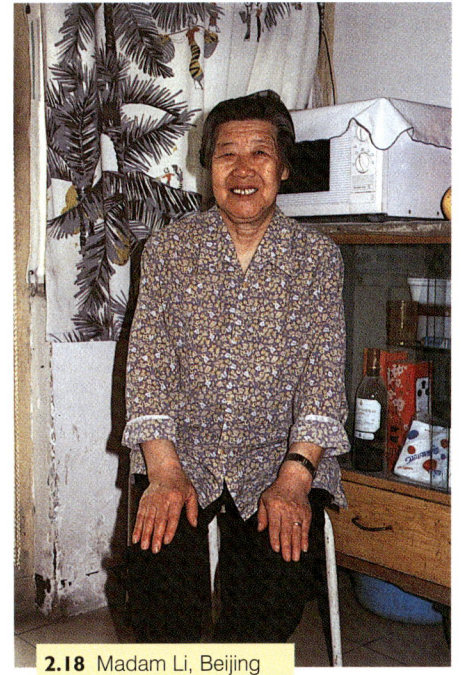

2.18 Madam Li, Beijing

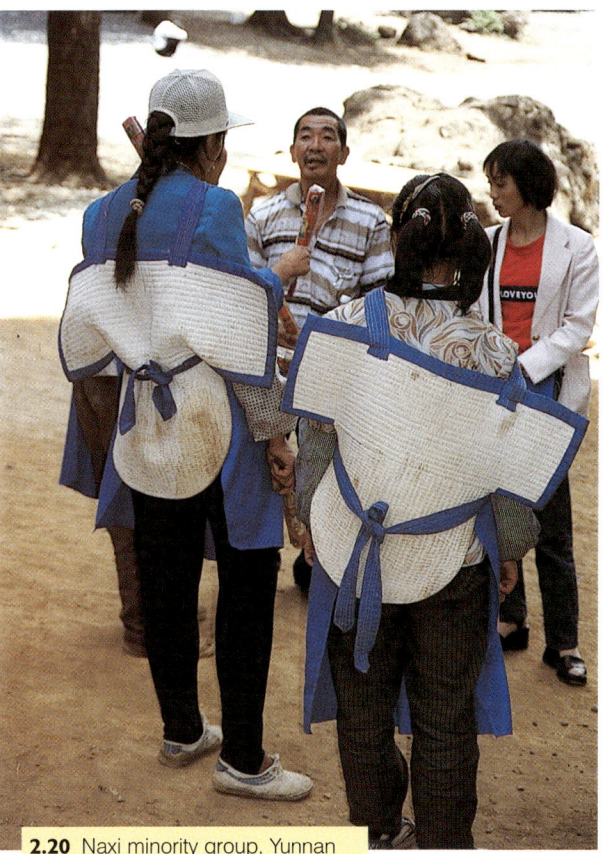

2.20 Naxi minority group, Yunnan

2.19 Dai minority group, Yunnan

bottom white, representing night and day, with seven embroidered circlets across its centre, representing the stars of the Big Dipper. When they are dressed like this, the women are ready to 'carry the burden of heaven on their back'. (In reality, the T-shaped apron helps to protect their back when they are carrying heavy baskets.)

3 Changing villages

Thurston — a suburbanised village in the UK

Many people still perceive a typical British village to be a self-contained unit in which a central 'green' is surrounded by such buildings as a church, public house and small shop/post office. The village may also contain a small primary school, and it is likely to include one or more working farms. To many people it is the ideal situation in which to rear children, or a place for retirement. Reality is often very different. No village stays the same for any length of time and no two villages are alike. This is because:
- villages change their shape and function over time
- some villages may grow in size while others decline
- the goods, amenities and services provided in villages change with demand
- accessibility (transport) may improve or decline.

Villages that are near to large urban areas, and which have good communications with those urban areas, are likely to be growing in size. Thurston, in Suffolk, is located some 5 km east of Bury St Edmunds (**3.1**). First mentioned in the Domesday Book of 1086, the original site of Thurston was at a crossroads south of St Peter's Church (**3.2a**). Until the coming of the railway in 1846, most residents were farmers or worked in local quarries. However, it was not until after the Second World War that the village began to grow rapidly (**3.3**), mainly because people were moving out of London. Many of the new residents were commuters who travelled to work daily, either by road or by rail, often as far as London. During the 1960s, the Heath was sold for housing, and the present-day A14 became a dual carriageway. In the 1980s, Malting Farm was sold for residential development.

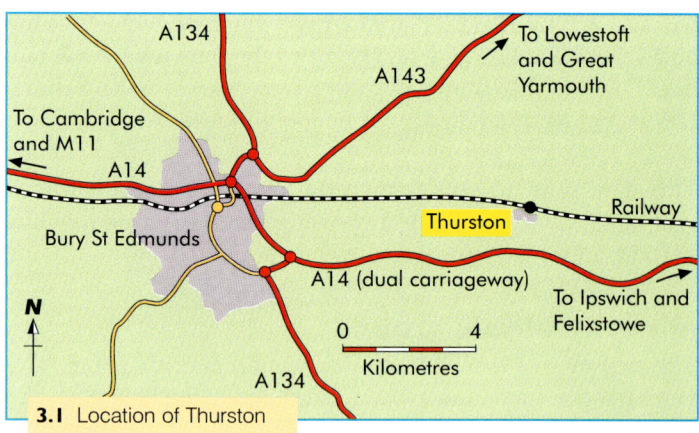

3.1 Location of Thurston

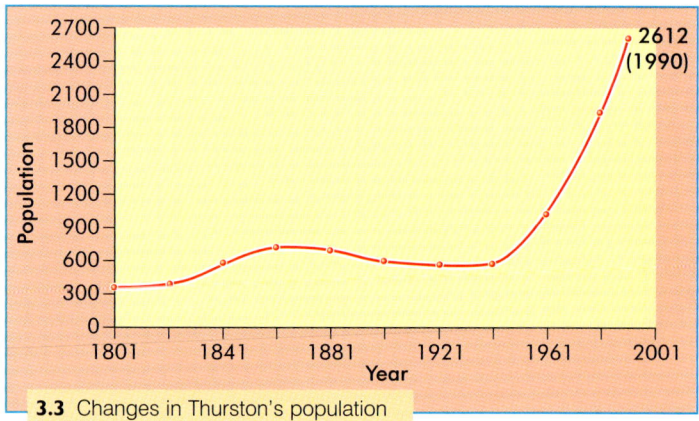

3.3 Changes in Thurston's population

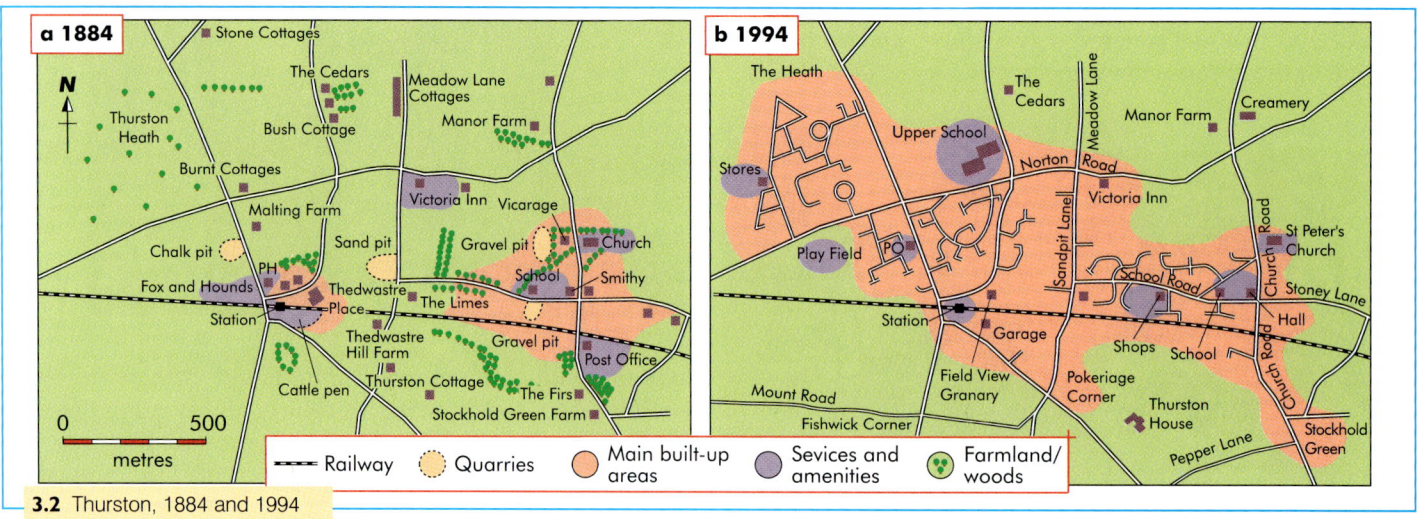

3.2 Thurston, 1884 and 1994

Figure **3.2b** shows some aspects of Thurston in 1994. Not only had it grown considerably in size since 1884, but it had, by adopting some of the characteristics of urban areas, become 'suburbanised'. Although the smithy and three of the named farms had disappeared, the village still retained its church, railway station, school, two public houses (see map and **3.4a**) and the post office (relocated, **3.4b**). However, several new amenities and services had been added (you should be able to name six), and there had been changes in both the function of the settlement and types of job available. Some of these changes are shown in **3.2**.

Figure **3.5** lists some of the changes that might result from the suburbanisation of a village. Benefits might include a larger school, more shops and other services, improvements in public transport, more local jobs and an increase in wealth. Problems are likely to include the upsetting, due to the influx of newcomers, of the social structure of the village, an increase in traffic and its associated problems (noise, safety and air pollution), a lack of affordable housing as house prices rise, and a loss of farmland and open space.

Which groups of people are likely to be in favour of and which groups against any future growth in the size of either Thurston or a village near to where you live? What would your preference be?

3.4 Thurston in 2000

a The village pub

b Relocated post office

Characteristic	Original village	Suburbanised village
Housing	Detached, stone-built houses/cottages with slate/thatch roofs; some farms, many over 200 years old; barns	Many new detached houses, semi-detached houses and bungalows; renovated barns and cottages; expensive estates
Population structure	An ageing population; most born in village; labouring/manual groups	Young/middle-aged married couples with children; very few born in village; professional/executive groups; some wealthy retired people
Employment	Farming and other primary activities (forestry, mining); low-paid local jobs	New light industry (high-tech and food processing); good salaries; local shops and transport
Transport	Bus service (limited); some cars; narrow, winding roads	Good bus service (unless reduced by private car); most families have one or two cars; improved roads
Services	Village shop; small junior school; public house; village hall; church	More shops; enlarged school; modern public houses/restaurants; garage
Community/Social	Close-knit community (many people were related)	Local community swamped; division between local people and newcomers; may be deserted during day (commuters absent)
Environment	Quiet, relatively pollution-free	Increase in noise and pollution, especially from traffic; loss of farmland/open space

3.5 Changes in a suburbanised village

Castleton – a village in a UK National Park

Castleton is a honeypot in the Peak District National Park (**3.6**). As such it faces the problem of balancing, at peak times, the needs of its local residents and the demands made by tourists, especially as the latter provide the major source of income. The village appears to be almost deserted at certain times of the week or year, yet is congested and overcrowded at others. This applies particularly to such amenities as the car and coach park and the public toilets, and to the volume of traffic in the main street. Figure **3.7** gives some of the findings of a survey, conducted in the late 1990s, on the amenities and services available to both residents and visitors. The survey did not show the number of second (i.e. holiday) homes.

3.6 Castleton from the air

3.8 Conserved houses in Castleton

The conservation of villages is an important task of the Peak District National Park Authority. The Authority is able to:
- control the erection of new buildings
- limit the range of building materials and allow only those that are appropriate to the local environment
- create conservation areas within the village, e.g. preserve buildings of historic or architectural interest (**3.8**)
- provide limited affordable housing for local people.

	Local residents	Visitors
Within village	**Adjacent villages of Hope and Hathersage**	
3 grocers/stores	Butcher	4 hotels
Post office	Baker	7 bed & breakfast
Police house	Chemist	4 camping/caravan sites
2 churches	Medical centre	Youth hostel
Village hall	Police station	Several second homes
Garage	Railway station	6 cafés
6 public houses		Numerous gift/souvenir shops
Fish & chip shop		Information centre
Library*		
Greengrocer*		

3.7 Amenities and services for local people and visitors

Mobile – once a week

Hennock, Rookhope and Longnor – villages in remote areas of the UK

A report published in 2000 claimed that of the 20 per cent (just over 10 million) of the population of England and Wales who resided in rural areas, 3 million lived below the poverty line. The problems of living in such areas include a lack of job opportunities, fewer services, and poor transport facilities (**3.9**). Employment is often limited to the shrinking primary industries, notably farming and mining, which are low-paid and lack future prospects. The cost of providing services to remote areas is high and there is often insufficient demand to keep the local shop, church, public house, bank or school open. With fewer inhabitants to use public transport, bus services decline or stop altogether. This forces people either to use their own cars or, if they can no longer drive or as petrol prices continue to rise, to move to more accessible areas. As a result of the process of rural depopulation, villages in more remote areas are often left with empty houses and an ageing and declining population.

Characteristic	Extreme rural (increasingly depopulated)
Housing	Poor housing lacking basic amenities; old stone houses, some derelict, some converted into holiday/second homes
Population structure	Mainly elderly/retired; born and lived all life locally; labouring/manual groups; young people have moved away
Employment	Low-paid; unemployment; farming jobs (declining if in marginal areas) and other primary activities; some tourist-related jobs
Transport	No public transport; poor roads
Services	Shop and school closed; perhaps a public house
Community/Social	A small community; more isolated
Environment	Quiet; increase in conserved areas (National Parks/forestry)

3.9 Characteristics of a remote village

Estimates suggest that 20 per cent of villages no longer have a bus service, while 40 per cent are without a shop and 50 per cent without a school. Many remote areas (**3.10**) have been designated Rural Development Areas (RDAs) whereby they receive government grants aimed at creating jobs, mainly in tourism and small-scale businesses, and in keeping the village alive.

Rookhope (North Pennines in Durham) Population of 800 in 1951 fell to 200 by 2000. Mainly due to decline in hill-farming and closure of fluorspar and lead mines. One bus a day other than school bus which takes children to nearby town. Lack of housing and work (one resident commutes over 110 km a day). Its own local report claimed the village to be 'a place of extreme social exclusion and deprivation with its residents at serious risk of becoming marginalised from mainstream life'.

Longnor (North Staffordshire) Young people moving out to find work. Increasing number of houses becoming second homes. Daily bus service to Buxton, but only once a week to Leek. Problems of visiting hospital, doctor and dentist. Village shop struggling to survive against urban supermarkets.

Hennock (Devon) Population of 1000 in 1861 fell to 250 by 1999. Two buses a week. Shop and post office closed. Public house up for sale. Farmers hit by fall in prices for beef, lamb and milk. Rise in house prices because in an area of attractive scenery (Dartmoor National Park).

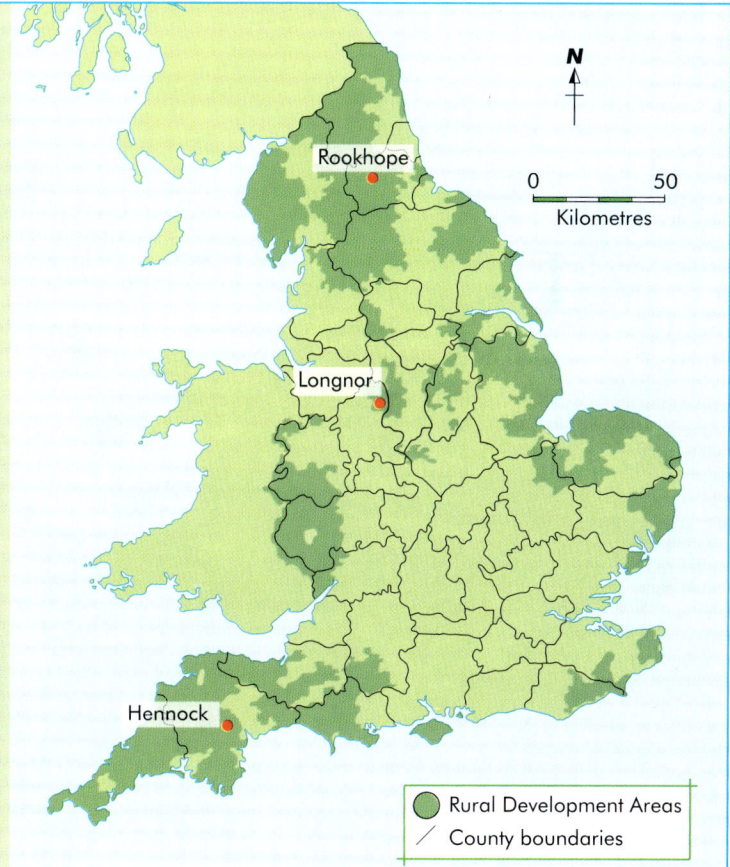

3.10 Rural Development Areas in England

Uti and Ooruttukala – villages in southern India

Villages in India are much larger than those in Britain. An Indian village, many of which are larger than some British towns, is defined as a place where over 75 per cent of the inhabitants are engaged in farming. Two villages typical of southern India are Uti in the state of Tamil Nadu and Ooruttukala in Kerala.

Most Indian villages are strung out along the main road (there is rarely a central point as in Britain). The road itself is likely to be dusty during the dry season and, lacking drains, flooded at times during the monsoon rains. It is often busy with old cars, cyclists, handcarts, trishaws and people (**3.11** and **3.12**). The street is lined on either side by shops which sell, in the main, local farm produce and processed goods (**3.13** and **3.14**). The walls of shops and houses are usually built with mud bricks which may, in some cases, be covered with a mixture of dried dung and mud. In Ooruttukala many of the roofs are made from palm fronds woven together, whereas in Uti they are more likely to consist of locally produced tiles (**3.14**, **3.15** and **3.16**). Corrugated iron is another roofing option, although this makes the inside of buildings very hot during summer and very noisy during rainstorms. Houses may have a veranda which gives protection from the hot sun and shelter from the heavy rain.

3.11 Village street scene

3.12 Road through a village

3.13 Village shops

3.14 Shops and shoppers

3.15 Housing – building materials

3.16 A backstreet scene

In the past, water has been drawn from the local river or stream but recently, mainly due to the help of international charity organisations, an increasing number of villages have acquired their own pump (**3.17**). The pump, with its reliable supply of clean water, has helped improve the health of many rural villages, and people no longer have to trek to the river for drinking water. However, rivers are still the main place for washing (**3.18**). The disposal of sewage is, and is likely to remain, a major problem. For fuel, many villagers have to rely upon local wood, palm fronds and crop waste. Some people use animal dung (which means it cannot be used on the fields as a fertiliser) or, if they are more wealthy, bottled gas. One recent innovation is the use of methane gas (a greenhouse gas): water is added to animal dung and the mixture is allowed to ferment in an underground tank. This produces methane, which can be piped to kitchens for use in cooking.

Hindus make up over 80 per cent of India's population. They believe the cow is a sacred animal. Westerners often find it strange that the animal is allowed to roam freely (**3.16**), but the cow provides energy to plough the fields and thresh the grain, and transport for people and their goods (the bullock cart). It provides dung for fuel (this is mixed with straw and dried before being burnt), as a fertiliser, and as a building material (mixed with mud it makes walls more stable and water-tight). It also provides milk. The cow is, therefore, much more valuable alive than in a beef-burger or curry!

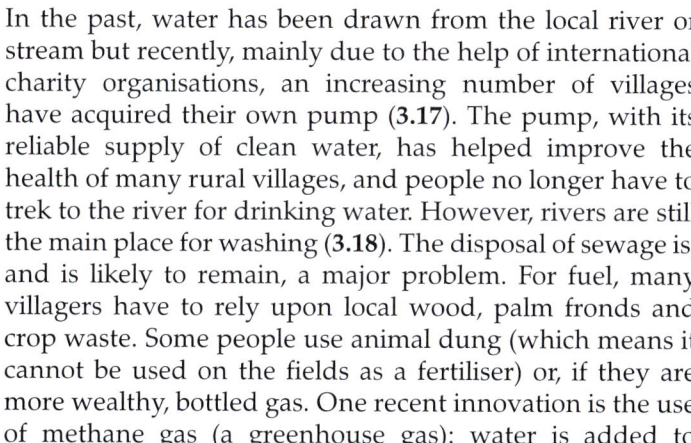

3.17 The village pump

3.18 Washing and drying clothes by the river

21

Hua Long – a village in Sichuan, central China

The village of Hua Long is situated in central China between the large cities of Chongqing and Chengdu (**2.11**). Like many other settlements in rural China, it dates back to the 16th century and experienced little change until the 1990s.

Most families in Hua Long are farmers, working long hours and living at a subsistence level. Many live in farmhouses grouped together, in typical Chinese fashion, around a central courtyard (**3.19**). Around this particular courtyard are 13 doors, signifying 13 families. The occupants have lived in these single-roomed dwellings for several generations (**6.5**). Despite the lack of running water, no means to dispose of sewage, and the presence of several pigs, there is no smell. The pigsty and several storage areas are built of mud blocks, but the houses are mainly wooden with tiled roofs. There are no chimneys and the openings, which serve as windows, have iron bars rather than glass. The centre of the courtyard is used to collect household waste for the pigs, for drying crops, for storing the limited amounts of farm equipment, and as a social meeting place. The farm shown in **3.19** was, in 1999, about to be pulled down. Although the families were sad to be losing their ancestral home, they were looking forward to living in modern brick-built houses with running water and electricity.

The Yang family, which includes two children (**2.13**), live in a large detached, two-year-old brick farmhouse on the outskirts of the village (**3.20**). Mr Yang has two jobs – working on his small farm, and operating a trishaw taxi in the nearby town of Dazu. His income enabled the family to save enough money, helped by a loan from his cousin, to replace their old wooden farm with a seven-roomed double-storeyed house. Apart from the kitchen (**3.21**) there is a living area and two bedrooms (all very sparsely furnished), and three rooms used for storing crops. Although the house has running water and a rather unsafe-looking electricity supply, it lacks sewerage.

3.20 A newly built farmhouse

3.19 Farmers' houses grouped around a central courtyard

3.21 The kitchen in the new farmhouse

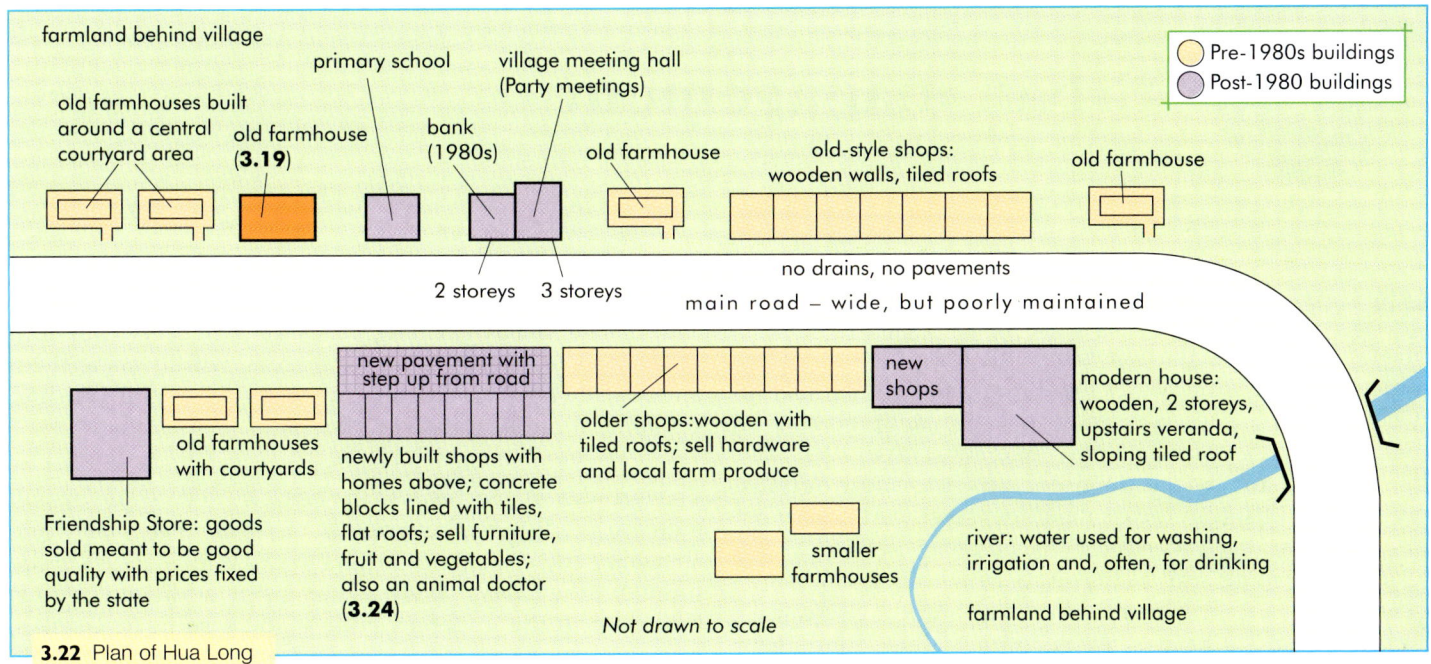

3.22 Plan of Hua Long

Hua Long itself is also undergoing change (**3.22**). It has a population of 2000, which is small by Chinese standards, and is linear in shape, with most of its buildings strung out either side of the main road (**3.23**). The road, only part of which has storm drains, is usually dusty and, despite its width, carries little traffic. Recent changes include the building of a bank (previously not needed as people were not allowed to earn money before 1979), an improved primary school (funded by a voluntary group that aims to improve education in the poorest parts of the country) and meeting hall, and a new Friendship Store. Along the main road are several modern tile-faced buildings with housing (for people re-housed from old farms) above lock-up shops and workplaces (**3.24**). Other new houses, some detached, indicate an increase in wealth of some of the villagers. Local people, although still very poor, claim that their qualty of life has improved in the last 20 years.

3.23 Buildings strung out along the main road

3.24 Modern shops and houses

23

4 Urban management

UK – traffic management

The rapid growth in the ownership and use of motor vehicles in developed countries since the 1950s, and more recently in developing countries, has led to major traffic problems in urban areas (14% of British households had a car in 1951, 72% in 2000). Traffic congestion, perhaps the most serious problem, results from the demand for travel, particularly by car, exceeding the capacity of the highway network. This results in queuing and delays on roads within, and linking, urban areas (**4.1**). The increase in road transport also causes accidents and difficulties for pedestrians (hindering their movement) as well as increasing the need for parking.

The greatest demand for parking occurs in central parts of urban areas and at major centres of employment, retailing and recreation. Allocating space for city centre parking poses a problem to local councils. As land values are highest in the CBD, councils can earn a much higher income by allowing land here to be used for shops or offices than they can for parking. Multi-storey car parks and on-street parking also create an adverse visual impact. On-street parking can also increase traffic congestion as it restricts the capacity (width) of roads and encourages vehicles to circulate as they look for parking spaces. Traffic problems are also compounded by unattractive and out-of-date public transport systems. Passengers face the discomfort of travelling, at peak times, in overcrowded trains and buses and, especially in south-east England, seemingly frequent delays and cancellations. The public transport operators, reacting to declining demand associated with increased car usage, economise by cutting less patronised services at non-peak times or, especially in rural areas, withdrawing them altogether. This results in an even less attractive and convenient public transport system.

The growth in car ownership has also led to an overall increase in distance between homes and places of work, shopping and recreation. Added to this is an increase in the number of journeys taken, as the cost of additional trips is low, despite the apparent endless increase in fuel prices, once the purchase, insurance and taxation of the vehicle have been completed.

As demands for greater mobility by an ever increasing number of people, both in Britain and across the world, continue to grow, so too does the need for improved traffic systems and more efficient forms of transport (**4.2**). However, improvements that appear to allow people this greater mobility invariably seem to have adverse effects upon the environment. Environmental problems resulting from traffic include health anxieties (e.g. asthma) caused by traffic-induced air pollution, and the nuisance of noise and the dangers of 'rat running' (traffic using residential areas as short-cuts or to avoid bottle-necks). The emission of greenhouse gases, from vehicle exhausts, is considered to be a significant factor in global warming.

4.1 Traffic congestion on a British motorway

4.2 Rail freight: containers on the move

The New Deal for transport means:	The Ten-year Transport Plan (July 2000)	
• cleaner air to breathe by tackling traffic fumes	£180 billion	one-third from private sector, two-thirds from public sector
• thriving town centres by cutting the stranglehold of traffic	£59 billion	on roads, including widening 580 km of roads, e.g. A1, M6, and 100 by-passes
• quality places to live where people are the priority	£60 billion	for railways, including 25 inner-city light railways and a London orbital railway
• increasing prosperity backed by a modern transport system	£26 billion	for local services
• reduced rural isolation by connecting people with services and increasing mobility	£35 billion	for other schemes
• easier and safer to walk and cycle		
• revitalised towns and cities through better town planning.		

4.3 The New Deal for transport in the UK, 1999

In 1998, the DoE (Department of the Environment) produced a document called 'A New Deal for Transport'. It began by stating:

'We want a transport system that meets the needs of people and businesses at an affordable cost and which produces better places in which to live and work. We want to cut congestion, improve our towns and cities and encourage vitality and diversity locally; helping to reduce the need to travel and avoid urban sprawl that has lengthened our journeys and consumed precious countryside.'

What the DoE wants for transport is shown in **4.3**. The document also spells out how the DoE sees its New Deal for Transport affecting both the motorist and the public transport passenger (**4.4**).

The DoE is looking at ways, such as taxation and tolls, to discourage car use, as well as framing measures to get freight transferred from road to rail. The Freight Transport Association (FTA) believes that 9000 fewer heavy lorries would be needed if vehicle size was increased to 44 tonnes. Although the government is said to be considering lorries of 41 tonnes, the FTA says that the larger size would be compatible with European lorries and that the extra axles (there would be six) would not cause extra wear and tear of the roads.

A major problem in adopting new transport systems in the UK is the time taken for their implementation. For example:
- The Channel Tunnel rail link was proposed in 1987, the eventual route virtually agreed in 1994, work began in 1998 with completion due in 2007.
- The British Airports Authority applied for permission to build a fifth terminal at Heathrow Airport in 1994, a public enquiry began in 1995 and lasted until 1999 with a decision not expected until 2002/3. The earliest completion date, if the scheme is accepted, will be 2010.

Compare these time-scales with those in Shanghai (pages 32–33) where there are no conservation groups, no public enquiries – and few safety regulations.

A New Deal for the motorist	A New Deal for the public transport passenger
• improved management of the trunk road network to reduce delays, through e.g. Regional Traffic Control Centres in England	• more and better buses and trains, with staff trained in customer care
• investment focused on improving reliability of journeys	• a stronger voice for the passenger
• better-maintained roads – increased resources both locally and nationally	• better information, before and when travelling, including a national public transport information system
• updated Highway Agency's Road User's Charter to give more emphasis to customer service	• better interchanges and better connections
• more help for the motorist if their car breaks down on a motorway	• enhanced networks with simplified fares and better marketing, including more through-ticketing and travelcards
• reducing the disruption caused by utilities' street works	• more reliable buses through priority measures and reduced congestion
• improved road safety and safer cars	• cash boost for rural transport
• quality information for the driver – before and during journeys	• half-price or lower fares for elderly people on buses
• dealing with car crime	• improved personal security when travelling
• more secure car parks	• easy-access public transport – helping disabled and elderly people, and making it easier for everyone to use
• better information and protection when buying a used car	
• action on 'cowboy' wheelclampers	
• more fuel-efficient cars	
• less congestion on our roads and less pollution by our cars	

4.4 The New Deal for the motorist and the public transport passenger

Lille – an integrated traffic system

Lille, with a population of just under 1 million, is the fourth largest city in France. It is located near to the Belgian border some 300 km north-east of Paris. Based on large local reserves of coal and smaller deposits of iron ore, Lille became the centre of a major industrial area in the 19th century. These resources led to the growth of the steel, engineering and textile industries. However, by the 1950s, as in other old industrial areas of western Europe, the region around Lille experienced rapid industrial decline. It was left with high levels of unemployment and large areas of derelict land, together with poor housing and inadequate modern services.

During the early 1980s the development of the French TGV high-speed rail network and the proposed Channel Tunnel rail link gave Lille an unrivalled opportunity to exploit its position as a focus for land-based transport. The city's mayor at that time fought against the original plan, which recommended that the new rail link should by-pass the city. Instead he persuaded French railways to build the new Lille-Europe station for the Eurostar trains in the centre of the city, rather than on the outskirts, on a site adjacent to the Lille-Flandres station which was already being used by regional and national trains (**4.5**). At the Gare Lille-Europe, a 400 m long window reveals both the TGV and the city centre (compare this with south-east England where local residents did all they could to divert Eurostar trains from urban areas).

The narrow-gauge VAL metro system, centred on the Gare Lille-Flandres, has two lines (**4.5**). The first line was opened in 1983. The second line, which has been in operation since 1989, was extended, and by 2000 Lille had the longest automatic metro system in the world. The tiny two-carriage computer-controlled trains run underground through the city centre (85 per cent of the total track) and on elevated tracks in the suburbs. They run at one-minute intervals during rush hours and at up to six-minute intervals at other times of the day. Energy-saving escalators only switch on when passengers step onto them. All metro tickets are single-fare and are issued from machines. The metro has no conductors and no ticket staff – just security cameras! The system safely transported 750 million passengers in its first 15 years.

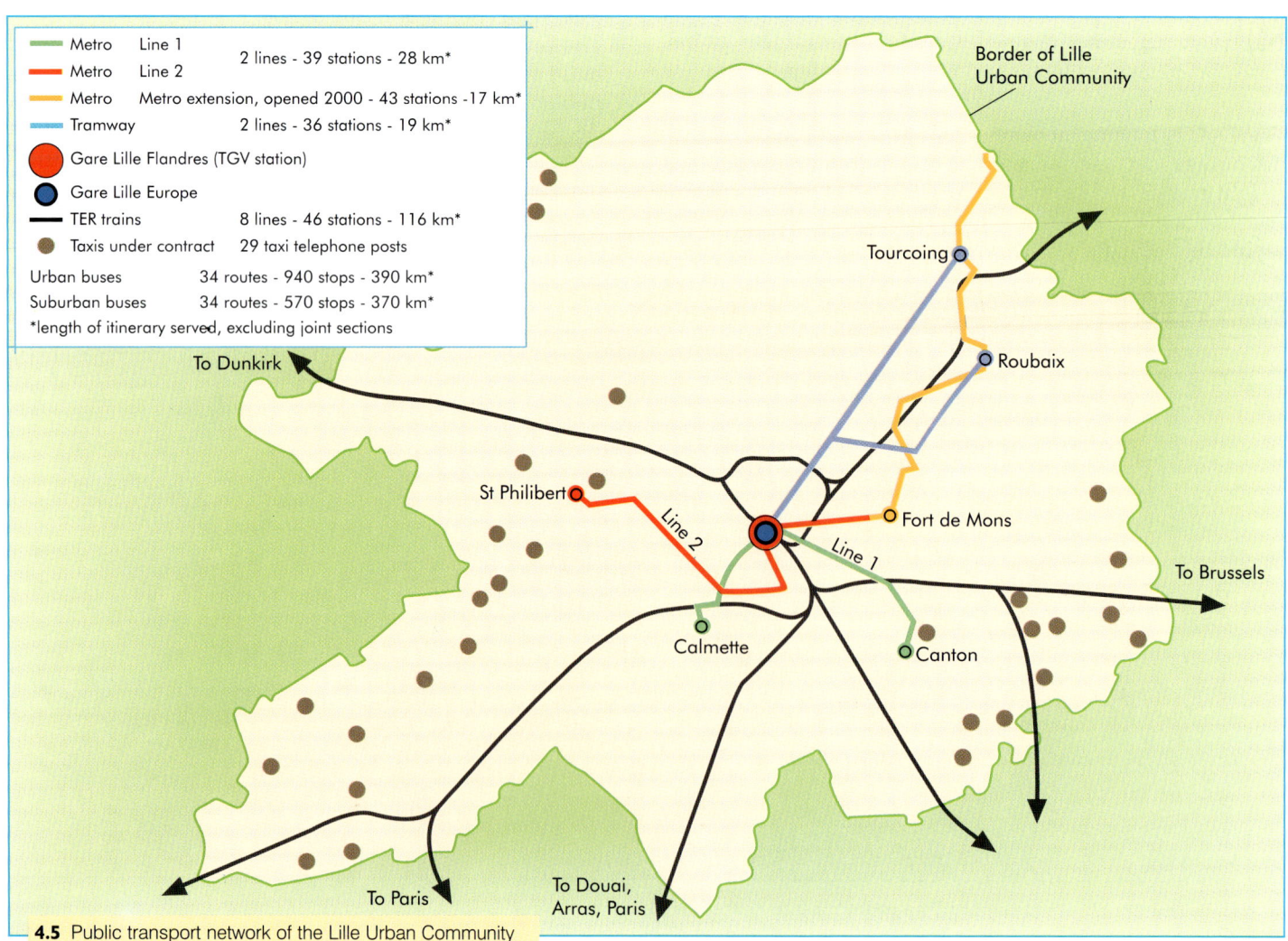

4.5 Public transport network of the Lille Urban Community

Above the TGV station are the twin business centre towers of the Crédit Lyonnais bank and the Lilleurope office block (**4.6**). Next to these, and bordered by an express highway which serves as an inner ring road, is the Euralille complex. Euralille has hotels, a large shopping centre (which includes Carrefour), an exhibition hall, a conference centre and a 5500 seat venue for rock concerts and other spectaculars. Around this complex are six car parks with spaces for over 6100 vehicles (**4.7**). Two tram routes, using newly designed coaches, run north-eastwards from the two main railway stations to the towns of Tourcoing and Roubaix (**4.5**). Residents also have the option of 34 urban and 34 suburban bus routes and, for those in the suburbs, access to a linking taxi service.

4.6 The two business centre towers: Credit Lyonnais (right) and Lilleurope (left)

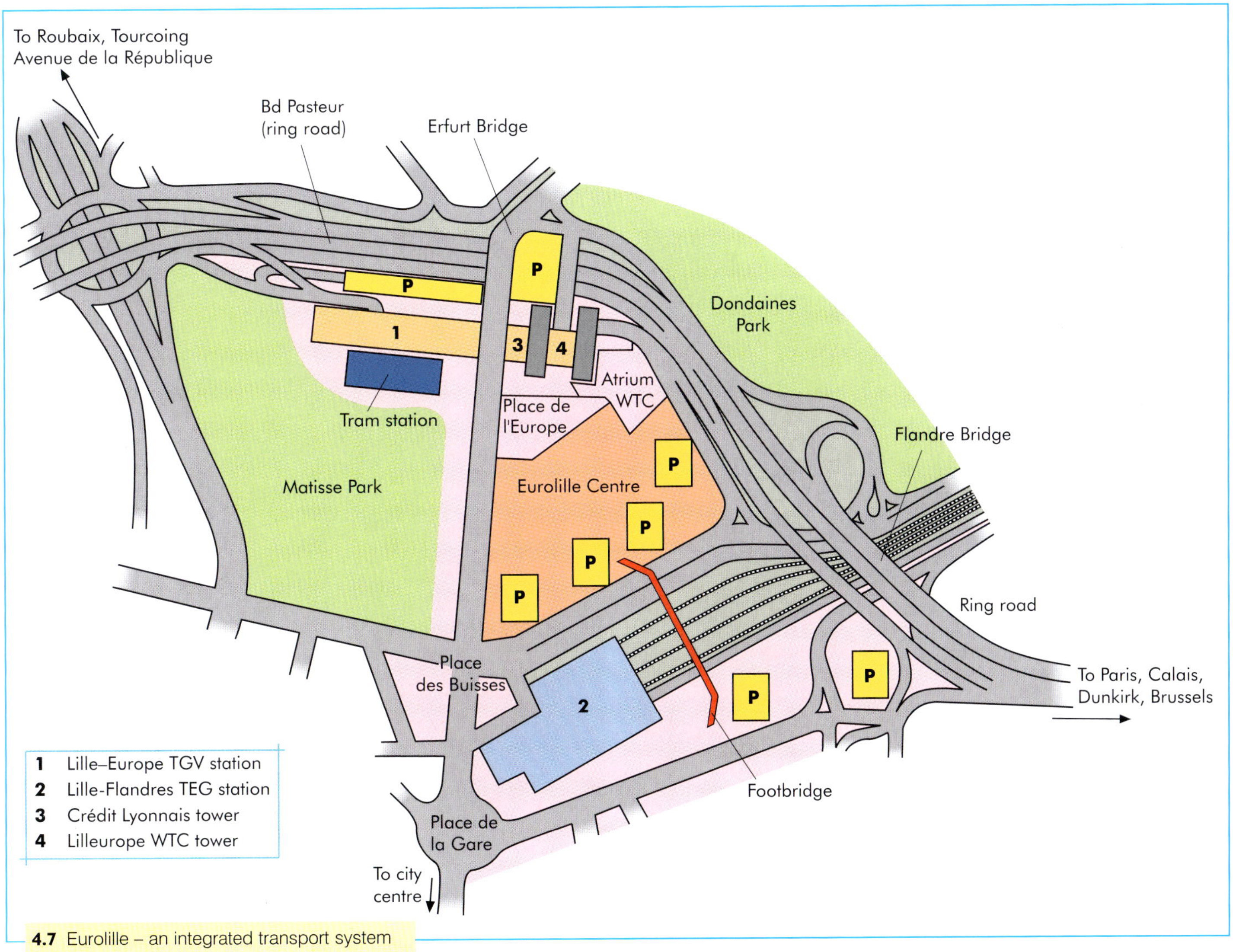

1. Lille–Europe TGV station
2. Lille-Flandres TEG station
3. Crédit Lyonnais tower
4. Lilleurope WTC tower

4.7 Eurolille – an integrated transport system

27

Jakarta – urban change in Indonesia

Jakarta, on the island of Java, is the capital of Indonesia. With a population of 11.5 million and extending across 40 km, it is the largest city in South-east Asia. Jakarta has long been an important port, exporting primary products such as timber and minerals. During the early 1990s, both the port and the city grew rapidly as Indonesia, taking advantage of its Pacific Rim location, began to develop new manufacturing industries. The city has attracted large transnational companies as well as becoming an important financial and business centre. As with other rapidly growing cities in developing countries before it, Jakarta is faced with numerous problems associated with urbanisation and rural–urban migration.

Some of these problems can be seen around Kuningan Junction, which lies at the edge of the so-called 'Golden Triangle' on the fringe of Jakarta's Central Business District (**4.8**). Until recently most of this area was occupied by a small residential settlement or *kampung*. Streets within *kampungs* are narrow and lack drains or pavements (**4.9**). They are flooded after heavy rain (Indonesia has a hot, wet equatorial climate) and dusty during drier periods. The houses are often two-roomed but, with a typical family size being 6 to 8 people, living conditions are cramped and uncomfortable (**4.10**). Some buildings are made from wood but many consist of earth blocks covered in a protective layer of lime, and most have a corrugated metal roof. Although the houses may have a limited electricity supply, very few have running water or a toilet. Water is obtained from a communal pump but it may well be polluted and, as it is obtained from underground, the water table is falling. Washing is done out-of-doors and residents have to pay rent.

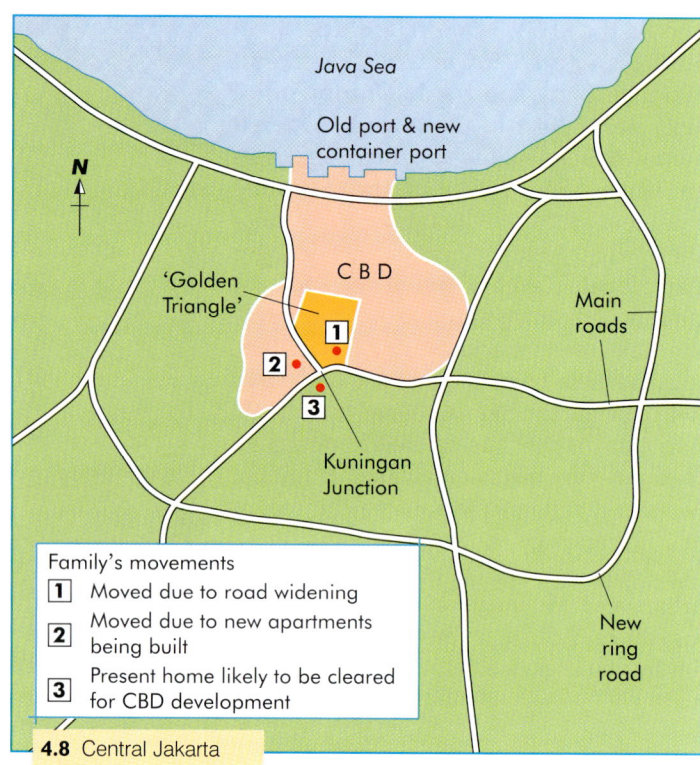

4.8 Central Jakarta

4.9 *Kampung* street scene, Jakarta

4.10 Inside a house in the *kampung*

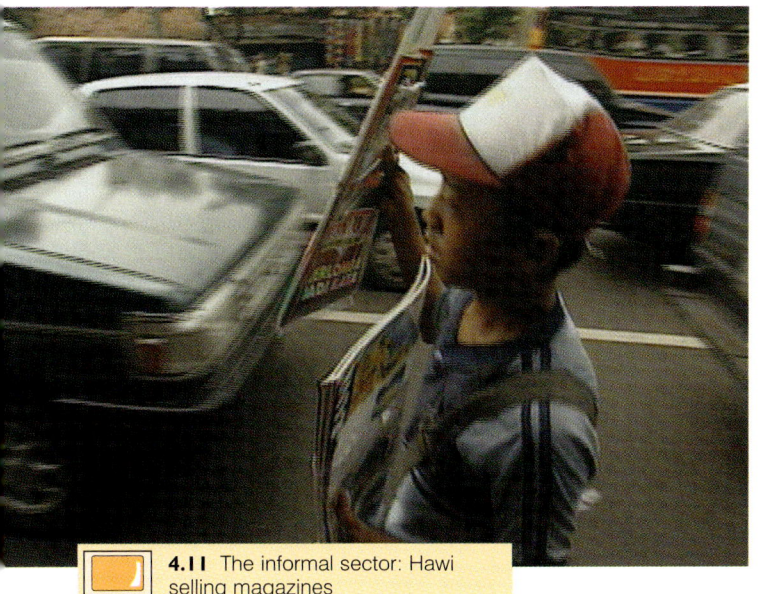

4.11 The informal sector: Hawi selling magazines

4.12 The formal sector: inside the Reebok shoe factory

Most of the residents find work in the informal sector. Some are able to open up the front of their houses to create small shops, while others find work on the streets selling items such as magazines (**4.11**), iced drinks and fruit, or cleaning shoes, reprocessing waste materials and repairing clothes or household items. Child labour is an important source of income for many families. Some residents find more permanent work with transnational companies such as Reebok. This workforce is expected to work long hours, often in an uncomfortable environment, for very little pay. Reebok, for example, in producing 22 000 pairs of training shoes per day, employs over 6000 people (who otherwise might not have a job) paying them (in 1997) £1.30 a day (**4.12**).

As Jakarta develops, *kampungs* such as that at Kuningan Junction are under continual pressure. For example, one family was forced to move when the land on which they lived was taken to widen the main road that bordered the 'Golden Triangle' into a dual carriageway, and again later when their new site was needed for high-rise apartment blocks (**4.8**). The family may well have to move again as land around them is being cleared for new office development. Figure **4.13** shows part of the 'Golden Triangle' with its financial, banking and office blocks, modern shopping complexes and urban motorways (but does not show the congestion nor the pollution).

4.13 Motorways and office blocks in the 'Golden Triangle'

29

Kunming – changing residential areas in a Chinese city

Kunming, which is the capital of the south-western state of Yunnan, has a population of 1.3 million. Until recently, and as in other Chinese cities, people tended to live in one of two main types of accommodation, both of which were small and likely to be overcrowded.

The most typical type was where several houses surrounded a central courtyard, as in the *hutongs* of Beijing or the *shikumen* (meaning literally 'stone-framed doors' which are found at the entrance to courtyards) in Shanghai. One such courtyard in Kunming (**4.14**) shows a round, central well with, to its right, an opening for the removal of sewage and waste water. The courtyard was surrounded on three sides by two-storey houses and, on the fourth, by a wall. The houses were made of wood and the roofs of either corrugated metal or tiles. The second floor had a veranda (**4.15**) which was protected from both heat and the heavy summer monsoon rain by an overhanging roof. It was usual for six to eight families to live in a building of this type. Although each house had two or three rooms, in earlier times, when the average family size was eight members (i.e. before the 'one-child policy', page 12), living conditions were crowded and unhealthy. Despite the greatly reduced family size of today, non-essentials still have to be stored out-of-doors.

The second type of housing was to be found alongside long, often narrow, streets where living accommodation was often on the first floor above shops and small work areas (**4.16**). As in **4.17**, the buildings often had a stone base, the ground floor was made of red earth bricks which were sometimes covered in rendering, and the upper floor either of red earth bricks or, more often, of wood. The small wooden windows contained glass, while the roofs were either made of earth (the poorest houses) or tiles. Today, electricity wires, in great numbers, hang everywhere and in seemingly dangerous positions.

4.14 Interior of a courtyard

4.15 Courtyard, veranda, and cramped living conditions

4.16 Building in an old street

4.17 Old street in Kunming

4.18 Old houses and early 1980s flats

4.19 Flats built in the late 1990s

By 1999, most of Kunming's older housing had been cleared and replaced. During a tour in 1999, a local guide claimed that most of this change had taken place in the previous few years, and that the courtyard shown in **4.14** (and in which he had lived as a student) was in one of only two such areas left in the entire city. As in other Chinese cities, most people living in Kunming now live in high-rise flats. These were originally built in the early 1980s:
- to accommodate the large number of rural migrants who were moving to urban areas to seek work
- when, following the introduction of the 'Responsibility System' in 1979, people were able to earn money which enabled them to afford better housing (**4.18**).

The most recent flats (**4.19**) reflect the growing affluence and rising standard of living, albeit from a very low base, of many urban dwellers.

The rate of change in Kunming was accelerated in order to modernise the city in time for the 1999 international Expo exhibition. Figure **4.20** shows the widened inner ring road thronged with cyclists and bordered by high-rise flats and ground-floor shops. The city's skyline is now very similar to others in many parts of the world (**4.21**).

4.20 The inner ring road

4.21 A modern urban landscape: Kunming's skyline in 1999

4.22 The old Chinese quarter

Shanghai – rapid urban change in China

The old, small and compact Chinese quarter in central Shanghai is one of the few remaining areas of extreme poverty and urban deprivation still found in that city (**4.22**). As in Kunming (pages 30–31), houses either flank narrow lanes or surround courtyards that are entered through stone-built doorways (*shikumen*). Houses are still built of wood. This, together with electricity wires that hang exposed along the streets, poses a serious fire risk. Although houses have electricity, they lack running water and an effective means of disposing of sewage and household waste. Living and working conditions, although not nearly as bad as they were two decades ago, are still poor.

During the late 1980s, most of Shanghai was shrouded under an almost continuous pall of yellow smog. This was mainly due to the widespread burning of coal and the increase in road transport. Coal was used for domestic purposes, in the growing number of small-scale work-units (the informal sector) and in several large-scale state-owned industries. Drastic problems, notably overcrowding, air pollution and traffic congestion, called for drastic solutions – solutions that would neither have been achieved nor accepted in Britain. This is because, in China:

- there are no public enquiries, and no conservation lobby (environmental protesters would not be tolerated)
- there is an abundance of cheap labour – people work for long hours and low wages, often without the protection of health and safety regulations.

In 1989, permission was given to develop Pudong, an area across the Huangpu River from Shanghai, which at that time was mainly farmland. Ten years later, Pudong was a large, modern city in its own right (**4.23**) with hardly any farmland remaining (**4.24**). Pudong is now a centre for commerce and finance (it has a new stock exchange) and also has large residential areas, restaurants and night-clubs, wide roads and numerous new industries (**4.25**). Many of these new industries are high-tech with, in 1999, over 5000 foreign-invested projects.

4.23 Pudong's new skyline, with the Pearl of Orient tower (on left)

4.24 New buildings and former farmland in Pudong, looking towards Shanghai across the Huangpu River

4.25 Modern Pudong

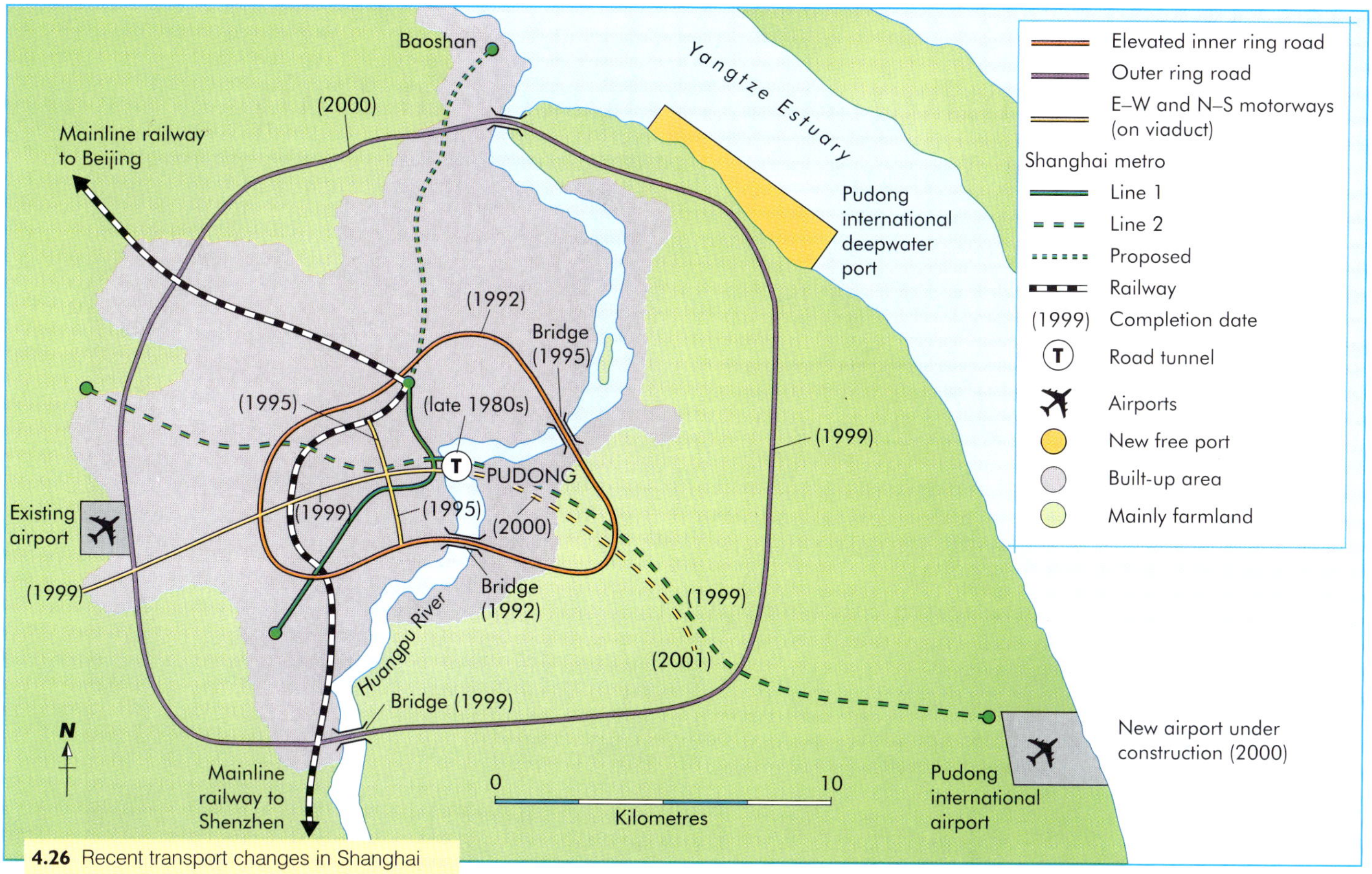

4.26 Recent transport changes in Shanghai

The first attempted traffic solution in Shanghai (**4.26**) was the building of a 47 km ring road, a project that took, from proposal to completion, less than three years. This was followed (1995) by a cross-city north–south motorway and (1999) by an east–west motorway. Each of these three-lane motorways, which were literally bulldozed straight through the city, has one carriageway built above the second (**4.27**). People living on these routes were given the option of being moved to a new flat on the suburbs, or being given money. While many were pleased to be relocated to high-rise flats with modern amenities, the new properties were often on the edge of Shanghai and a long way from people's place of work. Drivers, meanwhile, claimed (1999) that, in only ten years, average travel speeds within the city had doubled and atmospheric pollution had decreased considerably (though it still seems bad by British standards – **4.25**).

In 1989, the only method of crossing the Huangpu River was by ferry. By 1999 there were three road bridges, two underground (metro) tunnels and one road tunnel. Shanghai's first underground (16 km in length) opened in the mid-1990s, its second (14 km) in 1999, and two more are planned for 2001. A new international airport, east of

4.27 Elevated motorways, Shanghai

Pudong, was due to be operating by 1999, a second ring road and a 100 m wide, eight-lane expressway to the new airport were both due to be completed by 2000, and a new international deepwater port at the mouth of the Yangtze River in use by the early 21st century.

5 Farming and industry in Italy and India

Sicily – changes in farming in southern Italy

The province of Trapani, in western Sicily (**5.10**), is nearer to North Africa (200 km) than it is to Rome (900 km away) and Brussels (2800 km). It is a place where many ancient ways of life still survive. It has a harsh physical environment (climate, relief and soils) accentuated by its remoteness and adverse social factors (bureaucracy, the mafia and unemployment). Together these mean that the region has had difficulty in developing economically and in holding on to its own people – both factors have led to large-scale emigration.

Sicily has a Mediterranean climate. Although this means that winters are sufficiently mild (temperatures never drop below 12°C) and moist for vegetable crops to be grown, summers are extremely hot and dry with a drought that is long and severe. Between May and September, when crops need most moisture, rain rarely falls. By August, the land is parched (**5.1**) and most rivers have dried up. Only traditional drought-resistant Mediterranean crops, like olives and grapes, can cope with this climate.

There is also very little flat land, and the soil, apart from near the volcanic crater of Mount Etna in the north-east, is poor and stony. Deforestation, mainly by the Ancient Greeks and Romans, has led to extreme soil erosion (**5.2**). Sicily is also remote from the rest of Italy and Europe. Being an island presents other obstacles, notably the time (three days by road to Milan) and cost (shipping goods across the Strait of Messina to the mainland can double the farmers' expenditure) of transport.

Farming is still mainly labour intensive and badly paid (£2.85 per hour in 1998), and the feudal system of hiring labourers to work for absentee landlords (known as *latifundia*) remains in some areas. Farmworkers, regardless of whether they own their own land or work as labourers, usually live in hill-top villages and so have a long walk each day to their fields (**5.3**).

5.1 A large estate in a barren summer landscape

5.2 Soil erosion

5.3 A hilltop village in Trapani

5.4 Traditional method of cutting grapes

5.5 Modern method of collecting grapes

5.6 Modern irrigation

Figure 5.4 shows grapes being harvested, in the traditional way, by hand in Trapani. As the work is seasonal and the pay is poor, most farmworkers have to find a second job, e.g. supplying fuelwood or working in restaurants. Some of the larger farms, however, are now becoming increasingly mechanised. A grape-harvester, for example (5.5), can reduce costs by a half but, as it can do the work of 20 people, it increases unemployment in a region where over 30 per cent of those of working age have no full-time job.

Land reform in the 1970s did break up some of the larger estates. Since then, further changes have mainly been aimed at improving the environment or imposed by the EU.

- Environmental changes include afforestation and terracing of hillsides to stabilise the soil and reduce erosion, irrigation to conserve water, and crop diversification to reduce both monoculture and soil exhaustion. Irrigation has included the building of dams and the construction of drainage channels. Unfortunately in a region where 'who you know' and 'who can pay most' counts for much, it is the large landowners, rather than small-scale farmers, who are most likely to have a reliable water supply (5.6). Where the land is flatter, soils more fertile and water is available, farming has become more intensive and diversified (5.7). Greenhouses, which do not have to be heated in the mild winters, are used to grow flowers, household plants and tomatoes (5.8).
- The EU accepts Sicily as a marginal farming region. Although it has encouraged Sicilian farmers to enlarge their fields and become more mechanised, and has provided money for improvements in transport and irrigation, local people feel little real help has been given. They see little prospect of improving their standard of living.

5.7 Intensive farming with glasshouses

5.8 Houseplants growing under glass

35

Melfi – changes in industry in southern Italy

The Mezzogiorno, which means 'the land of the midday sun', lies south of Rome and includes the two islands of Sicily and Sardinia. It contains the poorest parts of the EU, with the region of Basilicata, which includes the town of Melfi, described in an EU report as 'the most disadvantaged of the 160 regions in the EU'. Figure **5.9a** gives some of the causes of poverty and high unemployment, and the reasons why so many people have emigrated either to the north of Italy or overseas. To this list can be added the lack of mineral and energy resources, industry, commerce, services and skilled labour.

In 1950 the Italian government set up the Cassa per il Mezzogiorno to try to develop the region. Initially money was spent on improving farming, roads and water supplies and later, to attract industry and tourism. Several large steelworks together with oil refineries, natural gas plants, car assembly plants, textile factories and steel and cement works were built. The scheme was replaced, in 1984, by two smaller agencies, one each for farming and industry. Today, despite government and EU aid and considerable environmental improvements (**5.9b**), the region remains poor by EU standards. Industrialists in the north appear to have became frustrated by the local population's apparent reluctance to change, and their lack of ambition, especially when they saw many of the new factories closing, to leave behind what have become known as 'cathedrals in the desert'.

The Fiat project

One big hope for the future has been the location of Fiat's most modern car factory at Melfi in northern Basilicata (**5.10**). When the company located here in 1993, it was seen as the south's last chance to obtain outside investment. Fiat located here (**5.11**) because of:
- lower labour costs
- lower land (and therefore rateable) values
- grants from both the Italian government and the EU
- a large pool of labour, some of which had become more skilled
- a more pleasant climate, especially in winter, than in the industrial north.

5.9 The Mezzogiorno in 1950 and 2000

a 1950

b 2000

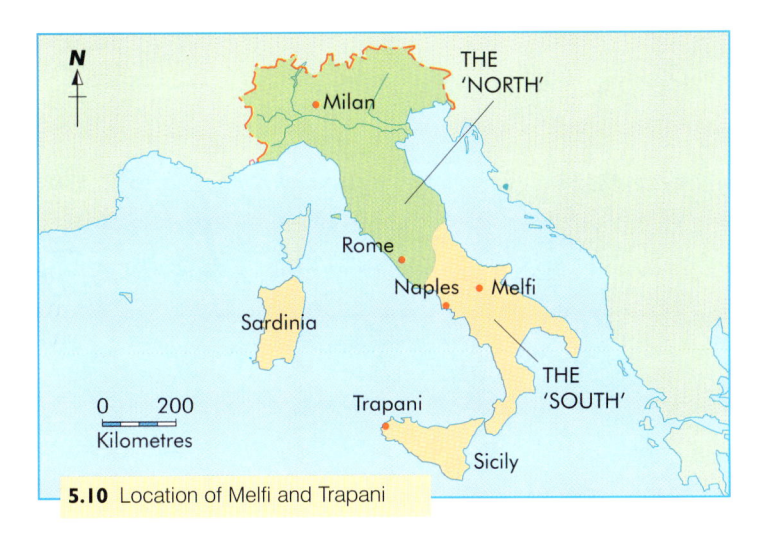

5.10 Location of Melfi and Trapani

5.11 Aerial view of the Fiat factory

The factory contains the latest technology (5.12). However, despite its highly automated production line complete with robots (5.13), it still employs 7000 local people, many of whom are young (the average age is 27). Fiat hopes that by employing local people, many of whom are well qualified, it can foster more modern attitudes to work and reduce the 'brain-drain' to the North. To date, the factory has not only reduced the flow of migrants to the North, it is actually attracting former migrants back to this region. This is mainly because, although wages are 30 per cent lower than in the North, the cost of living is also much lower.

Of the present workforce:
- most of the unmarried men still live with their parents
- many of the unmarried women, with a previously unknown independence, no longer accept that the woman's role is 'at home rearing children' (5.14)
- many live in surrounding towns and villages and, because these places have few job opportunities, have to commute (on company buses) long distances – some over 100 km (to those working on the 0600 hours shift, it can mean getting up at 3.30 in the morning, and a journey lasting up to two hours along poor and tortuous roads).

It seems that the Fiat programme is different from earlier initiatives as it was funded by private enterprise, not by the state. Private funders take care to ensure that their investments are secure. It is hoped that the success of Fiat will encourage the 'multiplier effect'. The multiplier effect is when a large firm, or a specialised type of industry, by being successful is able to attract other forms of economic development, creating jobs, services and wealth. In Melfi itself, the construction industry is already benefiting from a boom in house-building as the assumption is that many workers, who at present commute long distances, will want to live closer to their place of work, and with guaranteed wages will be able to afford better accommodation. Some young Fiat workers, as they gain self-confidence, are already expressing their ambition, as they acquire better skills and greater wealth, to open up their own factories.

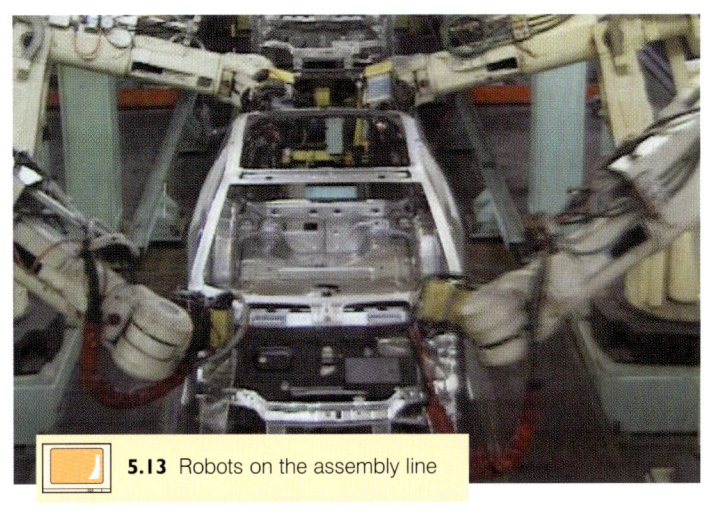

5.13 Robots on the assembly line

5.12 Inside the Fiat factory

5.14 Roberta: a modern, independent woman

Kerala – changes in farming in southern India

The village of Ooruttukala (5.15) is located near the southern tip of India in the state of Kerala (5.16). Kerala is one of the more wealthy Indian states. This is partly because its climate and soil are suited to agriculture, and partly because its government has encouraged the sharing out of wealth, mainly through education and social welfare.

Although rice is the basic food for most families in Southeast Asia, and India grows enough for its own needs, Kerala, despite ideal growing conditions, only produces one-quarter of its needs. Indeed, not only does Kerala have to import rice, mainly from the much poorer adjacent state of Tamil Nadu, but its annual production is actually declining. As in many other developing parts of the world, this is due to a conflict between the temptation and pressure to grow cash crops for export and the need to grow subsistence crops to feed the local people.

The summer monsoon rains arrive in early June and last until October. This, together with high annual temperatures and rich soil, enables two croppings (three with irrigation) of rice each year. Farming, traditionally at a subsistence level, is practised on small farms of under 10 hectares (ha). This is because, during the 1970s, the government forced landowners who owned more than that amount to sell their extra land. Each landless farmer was then given a plot large enough on which to build a house and with space to grow a few coconut trees and some vegetables (though usually insufficient to earn a living). Sasi, one landowner in Ooruttukala, grows rice on 2 ha, coconuts on another 2 ha, and bananas, tapioca and ginger on a further 4.5 ha. For most of the year he can manage by himself but at peak times, such as during the two or three rice harvests (5.17), he has to employ day labourers (usually the former landless farmers). Day labourers move daily from farm to farm but rarely find more than 15 days' work a month (5.18).

5.15 Main street of Ooruttukala

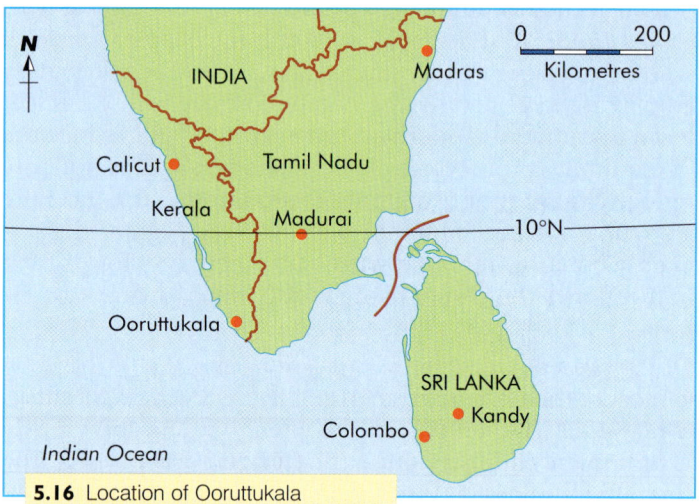

5.16 Location of Ooruttukala

5.17 Harvesting rice

5.18 Winnowing rice

	Rice	Coconuts
Growth	2 crops (3 if irrigation) a year	1 crop a year (7 years after planting)
Labour	Needs a lot of human labour; also some animals and machines	Needs some human labour
Inputs	Expensive seeds and pesticides, and fertiliser	Virtually no cost for seeds or pesticides, but expensive fertiliser
Output/income (value per ha)	3630 rupees	5330 rupees
Uses	Staple diet; straw for cattle fodder	*Liquid* is a milky drink; *kernels* can be eaten, dried or used to extract oil for cooking and cosmetics; *husks* for rope, mats and compost; *leaves* for thatching roofs; *palm fronds* can be used to provide energy; *residue* can be used for cattle fodder

5.20 Which crop – rice, or coconuts?

5.19 Cutting coconuts

Also during the 1970s, Kerala, like the rest of South-east Asia, experienced change during the 'Green Revolution'. This was when an improved strain of rice was introduced and yields rose sixfold. However, improved yields often led to the need for costly fertiliser and pesticides, and caused many of the poorer farmers either to fall into debt or to exhaust their soil – two problems mainly avoided in Kerala through better management. However, as Sasi claims, farming has changed. This is mainly because more information became available from the Department of Agriculture, a weekly farming programme was broadcast on TV, and the fact that the HYV (high-yielding variety) seeds and fertiliser were subsidised. So why, when Kerala is producing more rice per field, is there a decline in the amount that the state produces?

The answer is the increasing importance of coconuts which have now become Kerala's major cash (commercial) crop. Coconuts, once the tree has grown, are easier to look after and cheaper to cultivate than rice, earn 70 per cent more per ha than rice and have a greater range of uses (**5.19**). They grow best on dry land (also unlike rice) and can be inter-cropped with tapioca (an edible tuber – **5.21** and **5.22**) and bananas. Many farmers, including Sasi, have added soil to former padi fields so that they can grow dry-field crops. Venu, as a day labourer, is given six coconuts and 15 rupees for every 100 coconuts that he cuts (**5.20**). He prefers being paid in kind, as he can then sell or use the coconuts for himself and, as he gets them immediately, he does not have to wait for payment (as he must when payment is in cash).

Nevertheless, the government in Kerala is concerned at the fall in rice production. With all available farmland already in use, the government is trying to prevent any more land being taken out of rice production. To do this, it is encouraging small farmers (up to 80 in number) to group together to reduce their costs of production. So far this has made rice farming 50 per cent more profitable, but it has not solved the long-term problem.

5.21 Tapioca plant

5.22 Preparing tapioca for eating

Ahmadabad – changes in the textile industry in India

India is well known for its textiles. As early as 300 BC, people living near to the present-day city of Ahmadabad were exporting cotton cloth to Egypt. Today there is a huge demand for cotton garments in a country that has a hot climate, where each of the 1 billion people uses, on average, 14 metres of cloth a year, and where different kinds of cloth (especially for saris) are needed for different life-styles.

The first textile mills in Ahmadabad (which is 500 km north of Bombay) were built in the 1890s to compete with British factories. (At that time cotton grown in India was transported to Lancashire where it was turned into clothing before being exported back to India.) Ahmadabad was a good location as there were wealthy trading families here who were prepared to invest their money in new projects. Thousands of people moved to the city to find work in the textile mills, as the pay was better (even if the jobs were hard and repetitive) and they found the urban way of life easier than that of the village. Some families have worked in the mills for several generations. The industry grew even more rapidly after India's independence in 1947, mainly because the government protected it from foreign imports, passed laws that gave workers legal rights, and encouraged the payment of good wages. By the early 1970s, over 300 000 people in Ahmadabad were employed in 110 composite mills – i.e. mills where spinning (**5.23**), winding (**5.24**), weaving and the processing of cloth took place.

In contrast, villages across India in the 1970s were still manufacturing cotton cloth on hand- (and foot!) operated looms (**5.25**), as they had done for centuries. Here, men have traditionally done the weaving while the women spin and wind the yarn (**5.26**) – skills that have been handed down from generation to generation. By the early 20th century, the large composite mills were producing more cloth than the villages. Later, realising this, Mahatma Gandhi encouraged Indians to boycott cloth manufactured in the mills and to buy the cloth produced in the villages. After independence, the Indian government continued to help villages by allowing them to produce government uniforms. There are believed to be over 40 million handlooms still being worked in India today (**5.27**).

5.23 Spinning in a composite textile mill

5.24 Winding in a composite textile mill

5.25 Weaving in a small village

5.26 Spinning in the traditional way

5.27 Small-scale handloom operators

5.28 A 'sweat-shop' textile factory

During the 1980s the importance of the composite mills began to decline rapidly, for a variety of reasons:
- Synthetic fibres were introduced that were more hard-wearing, and also denim and new dyes.
- There was competition from small power-loom 'sweat-shop' factories (**5.28**). These are unregulated, have no protection by unions, pay very low wages, and workers have neither security (people are laid off when there is no work) nor holidays. This meant that they could produce cotton cloth cheaper than the composite mills.
- Composite mills suffered from high wage bills, a lack of investment, too much government regulation, poor management and a failure to adjust to changing tastes and fashions.
- The government had a policy of trying to restrict the production of synthetic fibres and, in aiming for self-sufficiency, ignoring the export market.

When the large Jubilee Mill closed in 1987, whole families became unemployed. Meanwhile, there was also a fall in the demand for village-made handloom cloth.

More recently:
- The few remaining composite mills in Ahmadabad have become highly mechanised (**5.29**). However, modern machinery, together with computers that assist at each stage of production, mean that far fewer workers are needed. Those with jobs within the main factory are extremely well paid, but most employees have to do contract work that is badly paid. A further problem is that very few school-leavers are being taken on.
- Women in nearby villages have organised their own self-employed association. They are adapting new schemes of work and introducing new styles, patterns and colours in saris (**5.30**). They also pass on their skills to other women in the village.

5.29 Inside a modern textile mill

5.30 A self-employed women's group making saris

6 Farming in China

China – farming types and changes in farming

In a country as large as China (see **1.1**), with its wide variation in rainfall (**1.2**), temperatures (**1.3**), and relief and soils (**1.6**), there are bound to be considerable differences in the types of farming (**6.2**, **6.3**, **6.4**). Generally speaking, travelling from south-east to north-west, the height of the land increases while temperatures, rainfall, and the length of both the growing season and the rainy season, all decrease. This means that, in very broad terms, six main types of farming can be recognised (**6.1**), five of which lie in the eastern part of the country. Notice also on **6.1** the two thicker lines:

1. The one in *black* forms a boundary between the drier pastoral country to the west and the wetter cultivated lands to the east
2. The one in *green* forms a boundary between the warmer, wetter south where rice is the main crop and the drier, cooler north where wheat and millet are the main crops.

Remember that the boundaries shown on **6.1** are very generalised, and there are many local variations and differences.

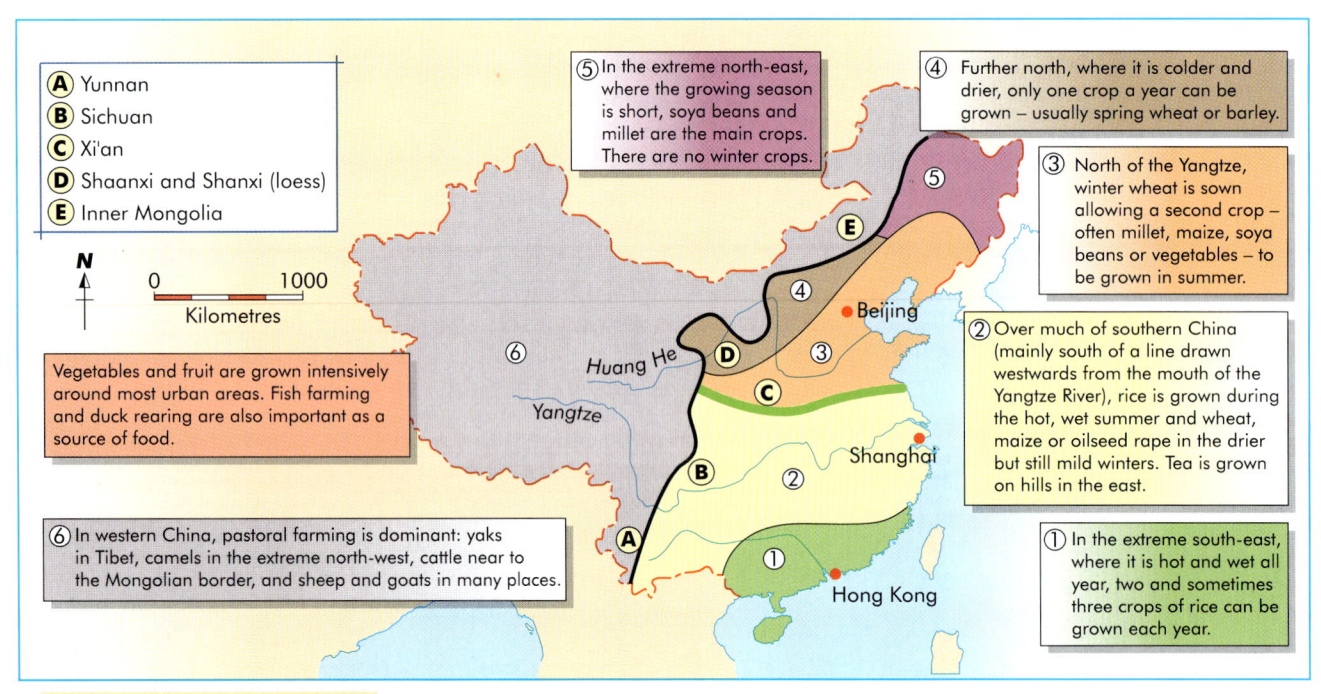

A Yunnan
B Sichuan
C Xi'an
D Shaanxi and Shanxi (loess)
E Inner Mongolia

Vegetables and fruit are grown intensively around most urban areas. Fish farming and duck rearing are also important as a source of food.

⑤ In the extreme north-east, where the growing season is short, soya beans and millet are the main crops. There are no winter crops.

④ Further north, where it is colder and drier, only one crop a year can be grown – usually spring wheat or barley.

③ North of the Yangtze, winter wheat is sown allowing a second crop – often millet, maize, soya beans or vegetables – to be grown in summer.

② Over much of southern China (mainly south of a line drawn westwards from the mouth of the Yangtze River), rice is grown during the hot, wet summer and wheat, maize or oilseed rape in the drier but still mild winters. Tea is grown on hills in the east.

⑥ In western China, pastoral farming is dominant: yaks in Tibet, camels in the extreme north-west, cattle near to the Mongolian border, and sheep and goats in many places.

① In the extreme south-east, where it is hot and wet all year, two and sometimes three crops of rice can be grown each year.

6.1 Main farming types in China

6.2 Camels in Inner Mongolia

6.3 Maize, wheat and fruit trees near Beijing

6.4 Rice terraces in Sichuan

Although there has been a significant population movement towards towns and cities and an increase in employment in the manufacturing and service sectors, 71 per cent of Chinese people still live in rural areas, and 73 per cent are farmers. Despite improvements both in farming and in rural settlements, most farmers still have a very hard life and live at, or just above, subsistence level. Many work in their fields from first light to dusk, relying mainly on hand labour (**6.6**). Although machinery is increasingly being used on the larger, flatter fields of the bigger farms in the north-east, animals such as the water buffalo (**6.11**) are better suited to the smaller fields and farms found towards the south of the country where every conceivable piece of land is intensively used (**6.8** and **6.9**).

The people's communes (1958)

After taking power in 1949, the communists under Mao Zedong confiscated land from the large owners and divided it amongst the peasants. One motive was the belief that collectivisation would increase productivity. After several experiments, none of which succeeded, the government created 'people's communes'. These were meant to become self-sufficient units, organised into a three-tier hierarchy and with communist officials directing all aspects of life and work. Each village commune was responsible for providing an adequate food supply (crops, livestock, fruit and fish), small-scale industry (mainly food processing and making farm implements), and organising housing and services (hospitals and schools). By the early 1970s it was realised that this system was also a failure, as it discouraged motivation and the use of local knowledge, did not allow people to earn money, and failed to increase food production sufficiently to meet China's then rapidly rising population. The farmers in **6.5** (see also **3.19**) were a remnant of the commune system, for although in 1999 they were about to be moved to new accommodation, their address was still Group 4 Team 1, Hua Long.

The 'responsibility system', 1979

This was a more flexible approach which encouraged farming families to become more 'responsible' (the commune system was finally abolished in 1982). Under it, individual farmers were given rent-free land in, or near to, their own village or district. The farmers then had to take out contracts with the government by which they had to deliver a fixed amount of produce. To help them meet this quota, individual farmers were given tools, seed and fertiliser. Once farmers had fulfilled their quotas, they could sell the remainder of their produce on the open market for their own profit. Farmers were also given the freedom to choose which crops to grow or animals to rear. The immediate effect, due to farmers having the incentive to work much harder, was an increase in yields by an average

6.5 Group 4 Team 1 – a remnant of the commune system in Hua Long, Sichuan

6.6 Today, under the 'responsibility system', farmers rent their land from the state and work it as a family (Sichuan)

of 6 per cent per year throughout the 1980s (**6.6**). Rural markets thrived, and some farmers have become quite wealthy (**3.20**). Profits have been used to buy better seed, improve water supplies and create village industries. Although most farmers have improved their standard of living, admittedly from a very low base, those living near to cities (a large local market) and in the south of the country (climatic advantages) have benefited the most.

1999

Hua Long, in Sichuan province (see pages 22 and 23), was one of several villages where residents claimed that their standard of living, quality of life and daily diet had improved considerably over the previous 20 years. Just as even the more rural of villages were showing signs of improvement in services and amenities (**3.22**, **3.23** and **3.24**), so the more efficient and prosperous farmers were also able to save money and to invest it in new homes (**3.20**) and machinery.

Sichuan and northern Yunnan – rice farming

Rice provides a staple diet for half of the world's population, including most people living in southern China (in the north, where it is too cold and dry for rice to grow, wheat is the staple food). The rice plant is a member of the grass family (**6.7**) and is native to South-east Asia. It is the seed and husk that forms the edible portion. It grows best where, during the growing season, temperatures are high and water is plentiful. Rice is usually grown in flooded padis with a hard subsoil to prevent seepage. In China, padis are of two types:

- Small fields on the flat alluvium-covered floodplain of a river (**6.8**). The padis are separated by small retaining walls, known as *bunds*, which have to be built to trap the floodwater that follows the onset of the heavy summer monsoon rains (compare the Ganges valley in India).
- Terraces on hillsides (**6.9**) which also have retaining walls, but this time to trap the rainfall itself (compare the Philippines and Bali).

6.7 Fully grown rice plants

6.8 Rice growing on the floodplain of a river near Kunming, Yunnan

6.9 Rice growing on a terraced hillside, Sichuan

Young rice plants are grown in a nursery (**6.10**). At the same time, the winter crop, which is usually wheat, maize or oilseed rape, is harvested and the fields are cleared. As soon as the monsoon rains fall and the padis are flooded, the men plough the fields with a wooden plough drawn by water buffalo (**6.11**). Although the soil is fertile, especially where silt and alluvium have been deposited by rivers in flood, fertiliser is added (perhaps only by the more wealthy farmers) to increase the yield (**6.12**) – a consequence of the Green Revolution (page 39). Meanwhile the women are collecting the young nursery plants and tying them in bundles ready to be transplanted in the prepared padis (**6.13**). Transplanting the rice, which is done by hand, is back-breaking work. During the time of the commune system, rows of women would work their way across the field (**6.14**). Today, under the responsibility system, it is more likely to be the farmer's wife working alone (**6.15**). The fields still need constant attention until harvest time. By then – September – the rains should have stopped and the padis dried out. Harvesting, using a small sickle, is also done by hand (**6.16**). Following the harvest, the rice has to be threshed (**6.17**) and the fields prepared either for a second crop of rice (if in the extreme south) or for the winter crops (in Sichuan) of wheat, maize and oilseed rape.

6.10 Young rice plants in a nursery

6.11 Ploughing with buffalo

6.12 Spreading fertiliser

6.13 Tying young plants in bundles ready for transplanting

6.14 A row of women transplanting rice

6.15 A single woman planting rice

6.16 Harvesting the rice

6.17 A hand threshing machine

45

Shaanxi and Shanxi – wheat, maize, and market gardening

The adjacent provinces of Shaanxi and Shanxi lie within the drainage basin of the Huang He (**6.1**). As far as agriculture is concerned, they have a harsh climate. Although summers can be very warm with temperatures above 30°C, the growing season is short. Winters, by contrast, are long and temperatures often fall to below –10°C. What makes the climate even more harsh is the lack of rainfall. Winters are very dry due to the prevailing winds blowing from the land (Siberia), and snowfall is fairly light. Summers have unreliable amounts of rainfall as the provinces are too far inland to gain the full benefit of the summer monsoon. Droughts are frequent – indeed it was during one such event in 1974 that a farmer, digging for water, accidentally discovered the terracotta army near to Xi'an in southern Shaanxi. When it does rain in summer, it often comes either as heavy downpours, giving surface runoff, or lighter rain, which percolates rapidly downwards into the porous soil.

The main characteristic of the region is its soil and relief (2B on **1.6**). The area is mainly a flat, featureless plateau averaging 1000 m above sea-level (**6.18**). Its surface is covered in a windblown deposit known as loess. Loess is a fine, yellow material that was blown from central Asia by prevailing winds at the end of the Ice Age. In parts of Shaanxi and Shanxi it is over 100 m deep, completely blanketing former hills and valleys. Loess has the advantage of giving a light, easily worked and very fertile soil but has the disadvantage of being easily eroded by wind and running water (**6.19**). Since the removal of trees and grass to allow cereal farming (mainly under the direction of Chairman Mao), the unconsolidated material has been washed away at a rate in excess of 1 cm a year. Estimates suggest that 1.6 billion tonnes of soil reach the Huang He river during the annual flood – hence its name meaning 'Yellow River'. For generations, many farming families in the region have lived in caves cut into the loess (**6.20** and **2.15**). These caves are cool in summer and warm in winter.

6.18 The loess plateau

6.19 Soil erosion on the loess plateau

6.20 Cave dwellings

6.21 Loess landscape in Shanxi in early May

6.22 Irrigation channel leading from a small reservoir, Shanxi

6.23 Irrigated crops in Shanxi

6.24 Extensive cereal growing (winter wheat) near Xi'an, Shaanxi

6.25 Intensive market gardening and a new farmhouse near Xi'an, Shaanxi

Across most of the region, the climate in winter is too dry and cold for crops. The land is prepared so that planting can be done in late May when temperatures rise and early summer showers arrive (**6.21**). Spring wheat (because it is planted in spring) and maize are the two main crops. With water supply always a problem, farmers have to rely upon irrigation (**6.22**). With an increase in wealth under the responsibility system, more farmers are able to afford to bring water, obtained from deep wells, to their land. Those with irrigation can grow vegetables and fruit (**6.23**).

In the extreme south, near to Xi'an (and the terracotta army), winters are less severe and rivers from nearby mountains provide a more reliable source of water for irrigation (**6.1**). Winter wheat (sown in late October) is grown in huge fields on an extensive scale. The crop, creating a 'prairie-like' landscape, is ready for harvesting in late May or early June (**6.24**). Maize, the usual summer crop, is then planted and is ready for harvesting in early October. Maize is more profitable than wheat, especially since the Green Revolution when new HYV seeds were introduced (page 39). In some places the newly planted maize is covered with polythene to conserve moisture and to encourage germination. Unlike most other parts of China, much of the work is done by machine. It is usual, within a village, for one farmer to buy (for example) a tractor, a second farmer a modern plough and a third farmer a combine harvester. However, whereas under the commune system each village shared the machinery, now each farmer can hire out what he owns. This enables him to make a small profit and helps him to pay for the machine.

Near to the large urban market of Xi'an, market gardening is important (and profitable). Shaanxi is the country's second largest producer of apples. Other fruit crops that do well include pomegranates, pears, peaches, apricots and, especially, strawberries, with peas and beans being the main vegetables. Here, the many new, large farmhouses reflect the increasing affluence of farmers under the responsibility system (**6.25**).

Northern Yunnan – Naxi farming

The south-western province of Yunnan is noted for its wealth of plants, and for being the home of almost half of China's ethnic minorities. The Naxi (page 15) live in the north-west, mainly in and around the town of Lijiang.

There is a considerable variation in climate across the province (the sixth largest in China). Although the south has a tropical climate, the east is more temperate (Kunming, the provincial capital, is known as the 'city of eternal spring'), and parts of the north-west are alpine (the Jade Dragon Snow Mountain appears in the background of **6.27** and **6.33**).

Over most of the northern half of Yunnan, summer lasts from May to August (**1.5**). Temperatures usually reach 25°C and there is plenty of rain associated with the summer monsoon. Winters are mild, with many places having a continual growing season, and dry. Temperatures are much lower in the mountains. Here snow may lie throughout the year on the higher peaks (**6.33**), while some valleys remain relatively dry due to the rainshadow effect (**6.26** and **6.27**).

Vegetation varies from tropical rainforest in the south, to temperate in the east, and alpine in the west. The province, widely referred to as the 'kingdom of plants', has over 18 000 species of larger plants and trees growing there. It is also the origin of many of the flowering plants and shrubs now found it Britain – rhododendrons, azaleas, orchids, roses and camellias. Yunnan has over 600 species of rhododendrons, and 650 of the 800 known varieties of azaleas. Other indigenous plants include bamboo, orange, kiwi fruit, camphor, tea, chillies and garlic.

During winter, the Naxi (page 15) are likely to grow barley, a crop that does not require much moisture, a few peas, or winter wheat. The barley is harvested by hand in early May, usually by women working alone in large open fields far from the village where they live (**6.26** and **6.27**). Water is obtained from runoff from the Jade Dragon Snow Mountain, although much of it flows underground. The land is then prepared for the main summer crop, which is maize. The Naxi family in **6.28** have two sons as, being members of a minority group, they were not subject to the rigid restrictions of the one-child policy that were imposed upon the majority Han population (page 13).

The field is first cleared of weeds and the soil then hoed into ridges and furrows. The ridges are watered, the water having to be brought some distance (from a small river) in a large barrel transported on an old wooden handcart. Polythene is then stretched over the ridges, soil piled onto the edges to keep it in place and slits made at intervals into which the young maize is planted. Polythene helps retain the moisture, encourages the seeds to grow and keeps down the growth of weeds. Within a few days, the maize grows to over half a metre in height (**6.29**) and is ready for harvesting in October. This part of Yunnan is too dry for rice.

In river valleys that have more rain and where the soil is more fertile, fruit and vegetables are grown intensively. The Naxi farmer living in the house in **6.30** is growing maize (centre left), beans and peas (foreground) and fruit, including apples and pears. Figure **6.31** shows some of the locally grown produce that is sold at a village market. Apart from fruit and vegetables – most of which we eat in Britain without realising that they are indigenous to Yunnan – several of the stalls sell a wide variety of nuts, including walnuts and peanuts.

Higher up, on the plateau, the land is used for crops that require little water and can survive in poor-quality soil. One such crop is vetch, a fodder crop that also adds nitrogen to the soil and whose purple flowers attract bees (**6.32** – note the hives). In the driest, rainshadow areas, beef cattle are grazed extensively on scrub vegetation (**6.33**).

6.26 Harvesting barley (early May)

6.27 Binding harvested barley

6.28 Planting maize

6.29 Maize two weeks after planting

6.30 Intensive market gardening

6.31 Local produce on sale at a village market

6.32 Vetch and beehives on the plateau above Lijiang

6.33 Cattle grazing on scrub below the Jade Dragon Snow Mountain

7 Industry in China

Changes and types of industry

When Mao Zedong (Chairman Mao) declared the People's Republic in 1949, China's economy was feudal with very little industrial development. Since then tremendous strides have been taken, although not all of them proved to be successful.

1953–58 The first 5-year plan This concentrated on developing labour-intensive industry, as labour was cheap and plentiful and machines were in short supply and expensive. Large state-owned factories, financed by the then Soviet Union and employing thousands of workers, were built to produce items such as iron and steel, chemicals, cement, textile and other machinery, ships, trains and armaments (7.1). Although industrial production increased rapidly, a cumbersome bureaucracy and over-centralisation led to inefficiency and a lack of personal incentive.

1958–66 The 'Great Leap Forward' This was the time when Chairman Mao tried to mobilise China's people and resources to meet often unrealistic production targets. Factory workers, like their counterparts in farming, were organised into self-supporting communes (page 43).

1966–79 The 'Cultural Revolution' In 1996, Chairman Mao set out to create a classless society. People who had previously been landowners (wealthy) or were well educated (teachers) were abused and sent to work on village communes. Many of China's works of art, including paintings, writings and buildings, were destroyed, mainly by the Red Guard. The 'non-cultural revolution', as one guide called it in 1999, virtually destroyed the country's economy.

7.1 Textile factory, Taiyuan, Shanxi

1979 to the present day In 1979, Chairman Deng Xiaopong replaced the commune system with the 'responsibility system', initially in farming (page 43) and later in industry. Encouragement was given to individual entrepreneurs who set up their own firms, especially if these produced consumer goods. At the same time, state-owned companies, which still accounted for 70 per cent of total firms, were allowed – once their more realistic production targets had been met – to sell surplus stock and to share any profit with their workers (e.g. the silk industry, pages 54–55).

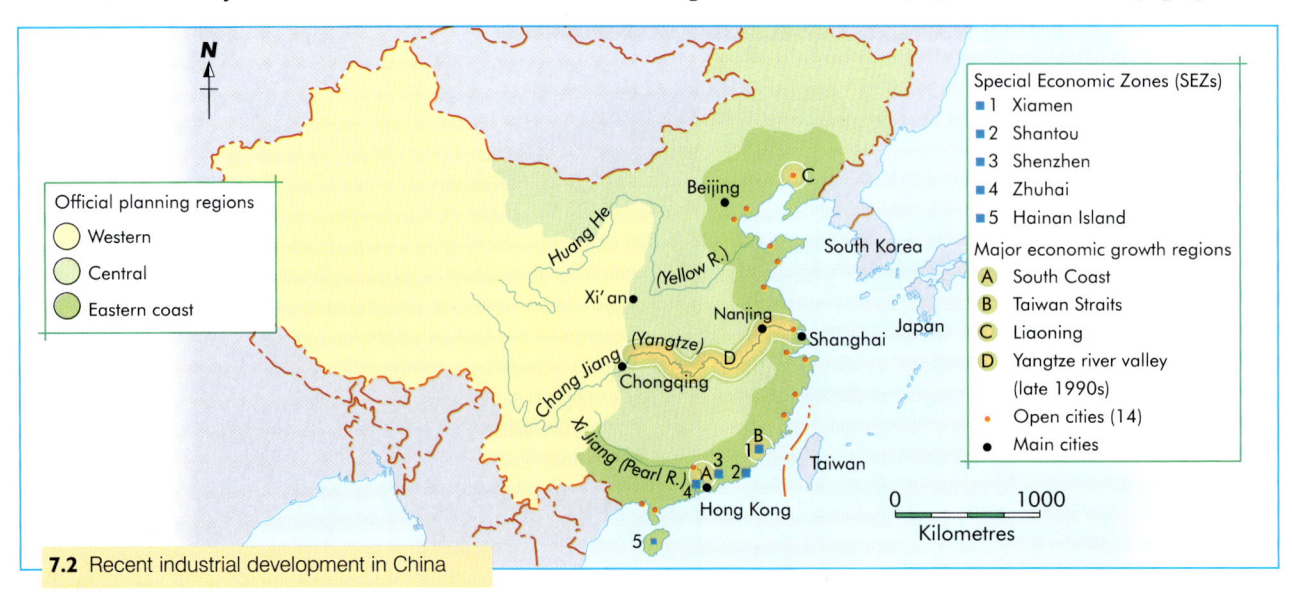

7.2 Recent industrial development in China

Later, attempts were made, with increasing success, to encourage overseas firms and foreign investment. In 1980 five Special Economic Zones (SEZs) were set up (**7.2**), including one at Shenzhen (pages 56–57). The SEZs integrate science and industry with trade. They benefit from preferential policies that facilitate exports and attract high-technology firms and other transnational companies. This was followed, in 1984, by the creation of 14 'open cities' that have the dual role of being 'windows opening to the outside world and radiators spreading economic development to an export-oriented economy'. In 1990, the Chinese opened several additional cities to overseas investment. These were located along the Yangtze from Pudong (pages 32–33) as far as Chongqing.

Types of industry

The following is a very broad classification of present-day industry in China:

- local industries making bricks (**7.3**), tiles, furniture and other domestic items, together with those that process farm produce
- craft industries, including those making items for export and the tourist trade, such as T-shirts, models of the terracotta army and copies of traditional paintings
- the informal sector which, as in many developing countries, includes large numbers of people often selling farm produce (**7.4**) or engaged in making or repairing goods and recycling previously used materials (**7.5**)
- old heavy industries, some of which are still-state owned and which often shed workers in large numbers due to their previous inefficiencies (**7.1** and **7.6**)
- township enterprises which are operated by villages and small towns (pages 52–55)
- high-tech industries which have been created mainly in the SEZs and open cities (pages 56–57).

7.3 Local industry – a brick kiln in northern Yunnan

7.4 Informal sector – street traders in Dazu, Sichuan

7.5 informal sector – a street tailor in Dazu, Sichuan

7.6 Factory on the banks of the Yangtze, near Chongqing, Sichuan

Xizhang – a township and village enterprise (Beibei Shoe Company)

When the responsibility system was introduced in 1982, entrepreneurs (individuals or groups of people) were encouraged to set up 'township and village enterprises' (TVEs) – a system unique to China. TVEs were formed, organised and run by people living in villages and small rural towns. Many were small in scale and used low-level technology. The TVEs soon created thousands of jobs, improving rural incomes and way of life (it is estimated that there are now 14 000 such enterprises employing over 20 per cent of the rural population). The increase in rural wealth led, in turn, to an increase in the demand for consumer goods. This resulted in many TVEs becoming 'joint ventures' by which they used capital from foreign investors who, wishing to produce goods for export to their own country, were attracted to China by its low wages. Together, the responsibility system, which encouraged maximum production, free markets and a greater incentive to work, and the success of many of the TVEs, led to the revival of the township as the basic form of local government instead of the discredited communes.

7.7 Beibei shoe factory, Xizhang

The Beibei Shoe Company is an example of a TVE (**7.7**). It is located at Xizhang, which in the 1970s was a poor rural district in Jiangsu province. Xizhang township is a two-hour drive north-west of Shanghai (**7.8**). It was formed in the 1970s when a group of farmers set up a small factory making parts, using rubber, for bicycles, e.g pedals and inner tubes. With so many people in China using bicycles (see **2.10**), the factory soon became very successful. During the early 1980s, and encouraged by the government, the company began both to expand and, by manufacturing rubber-soled shoes (at first for the Shanghai State Company but eventually on its own), to diversify. In time, following China's 'open door' policy, the company became a joint venture attracting overseas investment and technology, mainly from Taiwan and Japan. Despite the huge internal market for shoes within China, Beibei exports half its total output. In 1999, the company employed 2300 people and was producing 16 million pairs of shoes a year.

What were the advantages of locating at Xizhang? These were:
- a plentiful supply of local cheap labour (now supplemented by migrant workers)
- a good transport network
  - by road it is 2 hours to Shanghai and 4 hours to the new port at the mouth of the Yangtze (**4.26**)
  - by canal, along which raw materials such as rubber (from Malaysia), coal (400 km to the north) and cotton and leather (within 10 km) were brought and finished shoes moved out
- it is near to Shanghai for technical help, business connections and finance

7.8 Location of Xizhang and Suzhou

- it is near to Shanghai which is a huge local market and has port facilities, for exporting goods
- there was available space on which to build, and cheaper overheads than in Shanghai
- being near to Shanghai, it is possible to see new styles and fashions and to learn new techniques.

Most of the jobs in the factory are labour-intensive – the labour is cheap and, unlike expensive machines, can more easily adapt to new fashions and market demands (**7.9** and **7.10**). The success of the company as a large-scale employer has led to a shortage of labour in the area. This has meant that labourers from poorer and more remote rural areas are migrating here to work (rural–urban migration). However, while the increasingly wealthy local people are building large two- and three-storey houses for themselves (**7.11**), the migrants are forced to live in large dormitories where there is little space and amenities are few (**7.12**).

7.9 Men cutting out rubber soles

7.10 Women sewing together the upper parts of the shoe

Most local workers, who mainly make shoes for the domestic market, find the work repetitive and boring. They work reasonable hours (about 8 hours per day) and earn up to £50 a month. One girl, who can reach her home in a small nearby village in 10 minutes by scooter, lives in a house that was built, using bricks and cement, in 1989. Compared with her old house, which was made of straw and mud, the new house is large, light and clean. With all the family working at the factory, they have been able to afford the large house and such things as a washing machine, TV and fridge. The family admit that local people now live very comfortably.

7.11 New houses and washing facilities for local workers

Migrant workers, who make up one-third of the workforce, work in a different part of the factory from local people. They mainly produce shoes for export. One worker, who is a female supervisor, has only been home once (it is 200 km away) in two years. Migrant workers work very long hours (partly because there is little else to do) and can earn up to £75 a month by working a 14-hour day for six days a week. The female supervisor has to live in a single-sex dormitory, sharing a room with 10–12 girls. She has two lockable lockers (for her personal possessions) but no privacy. The communal washing area is shared by 60 girls (they 'go up the road' once a week for a shower). Despite the crowding and lack of amenities, other than a recreation room and a video, there is a friendly atmosphere here.

7.12 Dormitories and washing facilities for migrant workers

Suzhou – a silk factory

Silk production (sericulture) is dependent upon the silk moth and the mulberry tree. The first written record of silk was in 2640 BC, and came from China. Today, China still produces 70 per cent of the world's total, although the industry there has recently experienced problems, mainly due to overproduction and to competition from other fabrics (**7.13**).

Each silkworm lays 400 eggs at a time.
⇩
For commercial production, the tiny black eggs are kept on paper until, after 3 days, they hatch.
⇩
The baby silkworms are 3 mm in size – the same as a pinhead. They have huge appetites and are fed on mulberry leaves.
⇩
The silkworms grow rapidly, reaching 15 mm in 10 days (**7.14a**) and 65 mm in 25 days (**7.14b**), by which time they are fully grown.
⇩
Each worm then secretes a pale yellow gum into which it anchors its cocoon.
⇩
Within each cocoon either a single pupa (**7.15** foreground) or double pupae (**7.15** background) develop.
⇩
After a week, a silk moth emerges from its cocoon and the 40-day cycle is ready to begin again.

CHINA produces and exports 70 per cent of the world's silk, but has encountered unprecedented difficulties since the mid-1990s. As a result, the silk sector is being urged to reduce its surplus processing capacity and develop a number of competitive brands.

Yi Hui, Director of the State Cocoon and Silk Co-ordinating Group, said: 'The country will strictly control distribution of silkworm eggs and mulberry growing acreage to make sure cocoon production does not exceed 400 million kilograms in 1999.

Targets for 1999 aim at cutting the filature processing capacity by 36 per cent and the silk-spinning processing capacity by 28 per cent. This will mean cutting 190 000 spindles.

China should explore the domestic and global markets by cultivating a group of competitive silk brands, and divert funds to support research and development.'

Adapted from *China Daily*, 20 May 1999

7.13 Recent trends in Chinese silk production

The cocoons are then sent either to small township and village enterprises (page 52) or to larger factories in bigger cities such as Suzhou (**7.8**). The factory described opposite (**7.16**–**7.23**) is in Suzhou, which is less than two hours' drive north-west of Shanghai. This factory employs over 1000 people, most of whom are women, who work an eight-hour day with a half-hour lunch break.

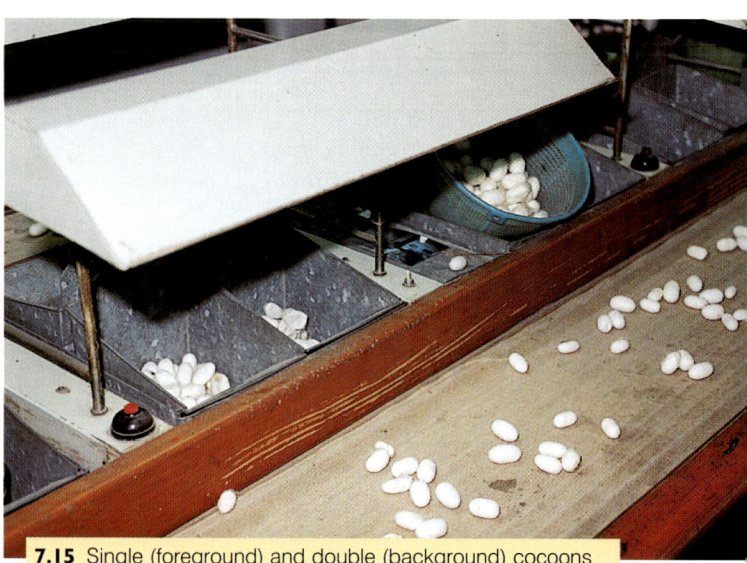

7.14 The growth of silkworms

a b

7.15 Single (foreground) and double (background) cocoons

COCOON WITH A SINGLE PUPA ← **SUZHOU SILK FACTORY** → COCOON WITH DOUBLE PUPAE

The single pupa, which is more valuable than double pupae, is immersed in boiling water for 20 minutes. This removes the gum and releases the end of the thread, which is located by one of a team of skilful female workers.

7.16

As they are transferred upwards, eight threads are spun into one larger thread which is collected onto a small six-sided spindle. Each cocoon can provide 1200 m of silk in spring, and 800 m in summer and autumn.

7.17

The spun silk is transferred to a larger winding-frame. Each female worker can spin 4 yarns, i.e. one frame a day.

7.18

The silk is used to produce high-quality garments such as those shown here. The factory is now able, under the responsibility system (page 50), to sell surplus stock.

7.19

The double pupae are also immersed in boiling water to remove the gum but, being double, the end of the thread cannot be found. Instead the cocoon is stretched out over a simple wooden frame to form a 'pouch'.

7.20

The pouches are hung up outside to dry.

7.21

Four women each take a dried pouch in turn and stretch it to the size of a single or double-sized duvet.

7.22

It takes 100 pouches, stretched out on top of each other, to make a double-sized duvet. The completed duvets are sold in the factory shop, elsewhere in China, and overseas.

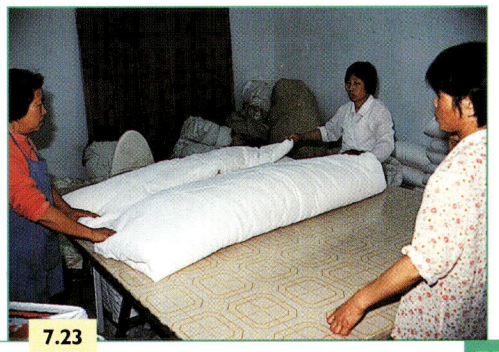

7.23

Shenzhen – high-tech industry in a Special Economic Zone (SEZ)

Shenzhen was designated in 1979 as a Special Economic Zone (SEZ – page 51). At that time it was a fishing village in a farming area and had a population – small by Chinese standards – of 30 000. Twenty years later, its population had risen to 3.8 million and only from the tops of the numerous high-rise office and residential blocks could the remnants of the former rural landscape be seen (**7.24**). Indeed as the population continues to increase by 250 000 per year, many parts of the city still resemble a huge construction site as more new offices, industrial parks, residential areas and urban motorways are built (**7.25**).

Shenzhen's rapid growth has resulted from a combination of factors, many connected with its location just across the border from the Hong Kong Special Administrative Region (**7.26**). Compared with Hong Kong, Shenzhen has:
- cheaper land values – its rents are less than half of those demanded in Hong Kong
- more space available for new industries and residential buildings – Hong Kong is very overcrowded
- a plentiful supply of labour, which is also much cheaper than that in Hong Kong and in other newly industrialised countries (NICs) in Asia
- financial incentives offered because it is an SEZ.

Shenzhen also had the advantages of:
- being close to the financial and commercial centre of Hong Kong
- having a coastal location that favours trade.

Shenzhen has become the most successful of China's five SEZs (**7.2**). Initially many of the early industries, including toys, textiles, tyres and electronics, were those relocating from Hong Kong. Later these were followed by transnational corporations that included Sanyo, Hitachi, Matsushita (all Japanese), Siemens (German), IBM and Microsoft (American) and Great Wall (Chinese). In 1998, the *Shenzhen Economic Daily* expressed concern over the increase and domination of foreign firms. By 1999 there were also 181 R&D (research and development) organisations within the city, and many scientific research and production firms that had developed strong links with inland universities. The present list of high-tech industries includes bio-engineering, medical science, and optical, electrical and mechanical integration technology (**7.27**). The annual output value of high-tech products made up one-third of Shenzhen's total industrial output and 90 per cent of its exports in 1999. Added to this, 40 per cent of China's wireless and cable telephones are made in Shenzhen.

7.24 Shenzhen – this was all farmland in 1979

7.25 Shenzhen in 1999

7.26 Shenzhen SEZ

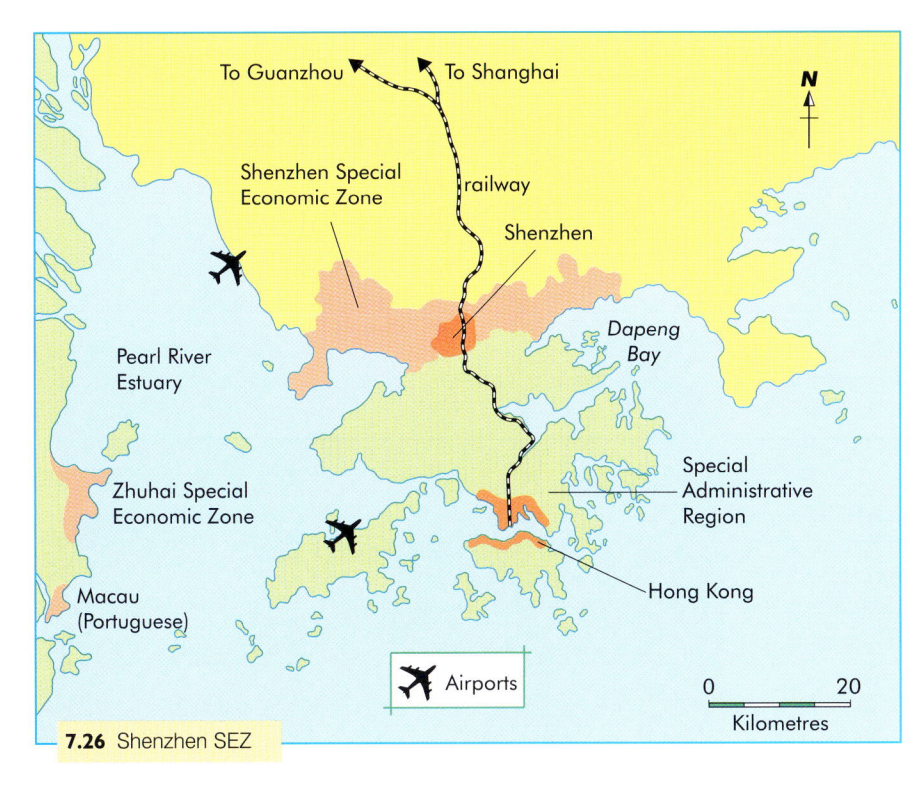

	National rank
Shenzhen Konka Electronics	4
Epson Technology	29
Shenzhen Nanyou	31
Uniden Electronics	42
Ricoh (Shenzhen)	44
Mawan Electric Power	48
999 Pharmaceutical	50

7.27 Leading Shenzhen companies

Many of the high-tech industries are located in one of four areas:
1 the Longan Grand Industrial Zone (covering 110 km²)
2 the High-tech Industrial Village (11 km²)
3 the Futian Central Zone (5 km²)
4 Cyber City (begun in May 1999).

Between them, the first three zones had developed, by 1999, over 2000 products.

Since 1980, Shenzhen's economic growth has risen, on average, by 20 per cent per year. By 1999 it had an income per capita of £420 compared with only £70 in rural China. This has meant a rapid rise in people's standard of living – as witnessed by the expensive high-rise apartments and the rooftop swimming pool visible in **7.28**. Shenzhen also has the highest car ownership in China (even if, at 4.6 per cent of households, it is low by Western standards). Figure **7.29**, taken from the top floor of the luxury Shangri-La Hotel, shows the main road leading to the railway station (the station looks more like a temple) with, to either side, large shopping complexes. The railway station is extremely busy as many people who work in Hong Kong live in Shenzhen (cheaper housing) and many Hong Kong residents shop in Shenzhen (cheaper goods). The green fields in the distance lie across the border in the Hong Kong Special Administrative Region.

7.28 Evidence of rising standards of living

7.29 Modern Shenzhen

8 Changes in energy

UK – wind farms

With the exception of hydro-electricity, wind power is the only renewable option being developed commercially in the UK. Even so, wind remains a vastly under-used energy resource.

As wind turbines are expensive to build and to maintain, it is an economic advantage to group a minimum of 25 machines together as a wind farm (**8.1**). Wind farms are best located:
- where winds are strong, steady and reliable or
- where the landscape is either high or the site is exposed, as on the coast, to the prevailing wind.

Individual turbines can stand over 30 m in height, have blades in excess of 35 m and, ideally, need to be 200 m from adjacent turbines.

Britain's first wind farm was at opened at Camelford in Cornwall in 1991. It was built on moorland 250 m above sea-level and where the average annual wind speed was 27 km/hr. It generates sufficient electricity for 3000 homes. By 2000, although there were 45 wind farms with 750 turbines in operation in the UK (**8.2**), wind only accounted for 0.2 per cent of Britain's energy need. There are currently more than 90 planning applications for the creation of new wind farms, and the British Wind Energy Association (BWEA) predicts that by 2010 there will be over 6600 turbines in the UK, many of which will be located offshore. They will then account for 6.2 per cent of the nation's energy needs.

Wind power has the advantage of being renewable and, by being pollution-free, it does not contribute to global warming and acid rain. Winds in the UK tend to blow more strongly and frequently in winter when demand for electricity is at its highest, and wind farms can create jobs in rural areas. However, environmentalists, including Friends of the Earth, the RSPB and the Countryside Commission, are not always united in their support for wind power. This is mainly because many of the actual and proposed wind farms are in areas of attractive scenery or important wildlife habitats. Elsewhere, local residents complain of noise and impaired radio and TV reception. Other people point to the fact that surplus energy generated during gales cannot be stored for use at times of calmer weather, and that it could take 7000 wind turbines to produce the same amount of electricity as one nuclear or conventional power station.

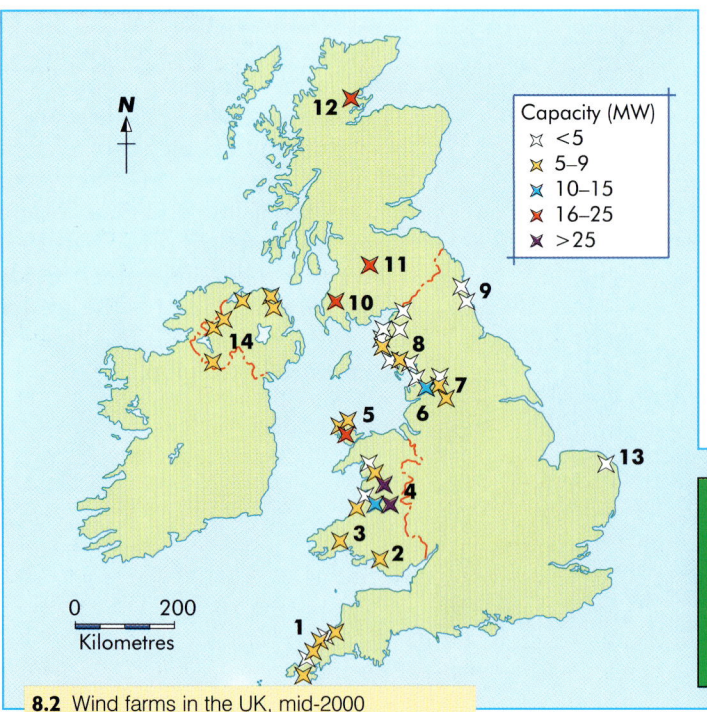

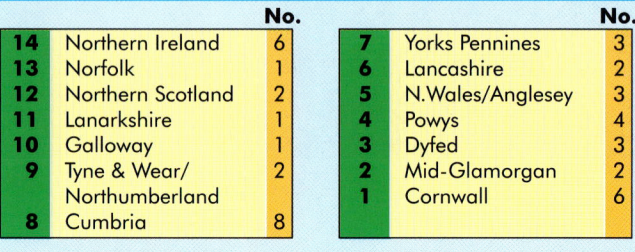

8.1 A wind farm in Camelford

8.2 Wind farms in the UK, mid-2000

		No.			No.
14	Northern Ireland	6	7	Yorks Pennines	3
13	Norfolk	1	6	Lancashire	2
12	Northern Scotland	2	5	N.Wales/Anglesey	3
11	Lanarkshire	1	4	Powys	4
10	Galloway	1	3	Dyfed	3
9	Tyne & Wear/Northumberland	2	2	Mid-Glamorgan	2
8	Cumbria	8	1	Cornwall	6

Capacity (MW)
- <5
- 5–9
- 10–15
- 16–25
- >25

The debate in Cumbria

Wind farms are beginning to change Cumbria's scenery. Between 1992 and 1999, 80 wind turbines were set up, and this number is expected to increase rapidly in the near future. Electricity companies have recently awarded contracts to developers for 15 new wind farms in the county, although, by mid-2000, approval had only been given for four of these.

Depending upon your viewpoint, wind farms either provide a vital source of clean, renewable energy, or they spoil the landscape for very little positive benefit. Country Guardian, an environmental group against wind farms, and the British Wind Energy Commission (BWEC), in favour of wind power, regularly update their respective Internet sites to discredit whatever is being said by the opposition (8.3).

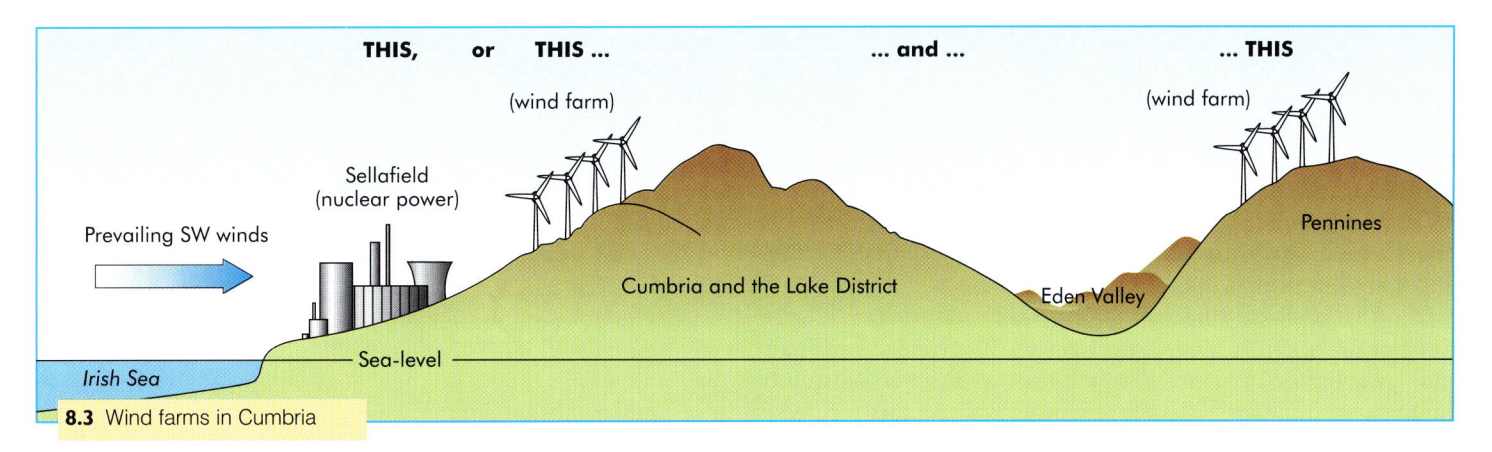

8.3 Wind farms in Cumbria

The views of BWEC	The views of Country Guardian
The UK has 40 per cent of Europe's wind. This provides clean energy, which will be needed when conventional power stations close down, as indeed many will have to in the next 30 years. There is no conspiracy to spoil the countryside. We just produce cheap electricity by putting turbines where it's windy, which is most of Cumbria. And wind turbines can be removed, unlike Sellafield. Visual impact is the only remaining issue and lots of people like turbines. You can't make them invisible, but how many people spend their time looking at them? What are you doing standing under a wind turbine unless you've got four legs and wool on your back? Country Guardian don't seem to realise that wind farms help keep the landscape looking the way it does at an ecological level by slowing down global warming. And many of the landscape features which people admire, such as hedgerows, fields and bridges, are man-made.	Of the 15 proposed new farms, three are in designated Areas of Outstanding Natural Beauty. Seven are on the fringes of the Lake District National Park. Dozens of turbines will be visible from places like Ullswater, Kirkstone Pass and Langdale. These turbines are massive. Some of them are half the height of Blackpool Tower. If you have them on the fringes of the Lake District then it's only a matter of time before they're on Helvellyn and Skiddaw. The developers would do it without any conscience. They'd walk away with vast, easy profits and we're left with the consequences. Wind farms are a gesture which allow politicians to say, 'Look at what we're doing for the environment'. But the tiny amounts of energy they produce do not justify that sacrifice (0.2 per cent). Wind developers claim to be acting out of concern for the environment. The truth is, they're only after the government subsidies. The wind farm companies are very powerful. They can afford to lobby politicians and organise expensive public relations exercises which put out misinformation. They're trying to change planning regulations to suit themselves. They embody the worst aspects of American-style big business.

Martin Dodds, the environmental planning officer for Cumbria County Council, becomes involved when district councils, which make the decision on wind farm applications, ask the county council for advice. The number of applications is increasing due to the government's Non-Fossil Fuel Obligation, by which electricity companies have to buy an increasing amount of their energy from renewable sources such as wind. According to Mr Dodds:

'Most objections to wind farms are lodged on the grounds of visibility and noise. Proximity to a National Park is a factor, but not grounds for a refusal. Each case is taken on merit. We will support proposals where there are no adverse consequences or where the disadvantages are outweighed by benefits. We weigh up, and balance, factors like energy implications and the visual impact.'

China – from coal to hydro-electricity

In the mid-1990s, most of China's energy came from coal. This was not surprising considering that China was mining, each year, two-fifths of the world's total. Coal is mined in most parts of the country, although production is greatest to the north of the Yangtze River (**8.4**) and least in the mountains and deserts in the west of the country. Coal, which accounted for 75 per cent of the country's energy consumption, was the engine of the country's economic development. It was used to light China's streets, cook its food, run its power stations and factories (**8.5**) and – where people could afford it – to heat their homes (**8.6**). Unfortunately, because coal was cheap to mine and found in abundant quantities, it was used inefficiently. The result was severe atmospheric pollution in many Chinese cities (**8.7**), acid rain over much of the country, and the release of carbon dioxide. (Although China was blamed for 10 per cent of the world's greenhouse gases, this was far less than the percentage contribution by the USA with its much smaller population.) By 1995, China had 35 large power stations – 26 thermal, 7 hydro-electric (the largest being at Gezhouba on the Yangtze) and 2 nuclear.

By 2000, several major changes were taking place. One reason for this change was a growing concern within the country as to the possible effects of global warming. For example:
- According to the UN, rising sea-levels could result in up to 70 million people living in coastal areas, including Shanghai, Tianjin and Guanzhou, losing their homes.
- The Chinese themselves have witnessed changes in their climate that have resulted in more typhoons (pages 68–69), an increase in flooding in the Yangtze basin (pages 74–75), and severe drought in the Huang He basin.

To reduce pollution levels, the Chinese are closing large numbers of small and inefficient coal mines (over 25 000 in 1999 alone) and reducing coal production (by 250 million tonnes in 1999). The use of oil has increased and there are plans to use more natural gas and to produce more nuclear power. However, the biggest change is likely to come after 2003 when hydro-electricity becomes available from the huge and controversial Three Gorges Dam on the Yangtze River.

8.4 Anthracite coal mine in Shaanxi

8.5 Coal-burning factory beside the Yangtze River

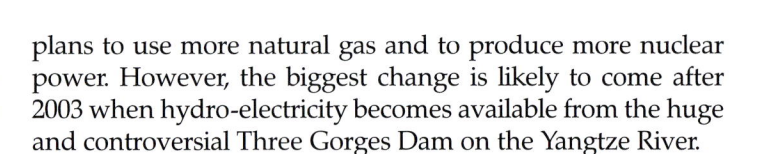

8.6 Briquettes made from compressed coal and oil, for domestic use

8.7 Air pollution in Chengdu

8.8 The Three Gorges Project

The Three Gorges Dam

On either side of the spillway, at the toe of the dam, two large power stations are being built (**8.8**). The power station nearer the south bank will have 12 generators, the one nearer the north bank 14 generators (**8.9** shows the installation of two of the turbines in May 1999). Each of the 26 generators will produce 680 MW, giving a combined total of 17 680 MW). The electricity will then be transferred for use in central China, eastern China (including Shanghai and Pudong – pages 32 and 33) and, to the west, eastern Sichuan (Chongqing).

Electricity from the Three Gorges will save 40 million tonnes of coal a year. It will end the energy shortage in central and eastern China and will encourage economic development along the Yangtze from Chongqing to Shanghai (**8.10**). In terms of supplying energy, hydro-electricity is a clean and renewable form of energy and its production will reduce the amount of coal being burnt and, consequently, levels of pollution within China, and global warming internationally. However, many environmentalists in the Western world are opposed to the Three Gorges Project (pages 92 and 93).

8.9 Installing three turbines (May 1999)

8.10 New high-tech industry in Yichang, near the Three Gorges Dam

9 Hazards

Austria – avalanches

An avalanche is a sudden downhill movement of snow, ice and/or rock (**9.1**) It occurs when the weight of loose material on a valley side becomes sufficient to overcome friction. This allows the material to descend at considerable speed under the force of gravity (an example of mass movement). The average speed of descent is 40–60 km/hr but video recordings have shown they can exceed 200 km/hr.

Austria, February 1999

Villages, hamlets and alpine resorts in western Austria have been built in places that, in the past, had proved to be safe from avalanches. After several years of relatively light snowfalls, the winter of 1998/99 gave many places their heaviest falls of the century. By mid-February, local experts were claiming that the avalanche risk was greater than it had been in living memory. Some of the first victims were people who strayed off-piste into danger zones. Later, following further heavy snowfalls, the victims were tourists and residents in their chalets and houses – places normally considered to be the safest in times of avalanches.

What made February 1999 different was an unusual sequence of events. These began with a milder spell of weather with temperatures high enough for rain to fall on the lower slopes. When temperatures fell again, the rain gave way to snow and froze. Poor visibility then prevented controlled avalanches being set off by high explosives (a method used to dissipate the avalanche danger). The sequence ended when further heavy snowfalls, falling onto an icy base, were whipped up by winds of up to 120 km/hr and which blew from an unusual north-westerly direction.

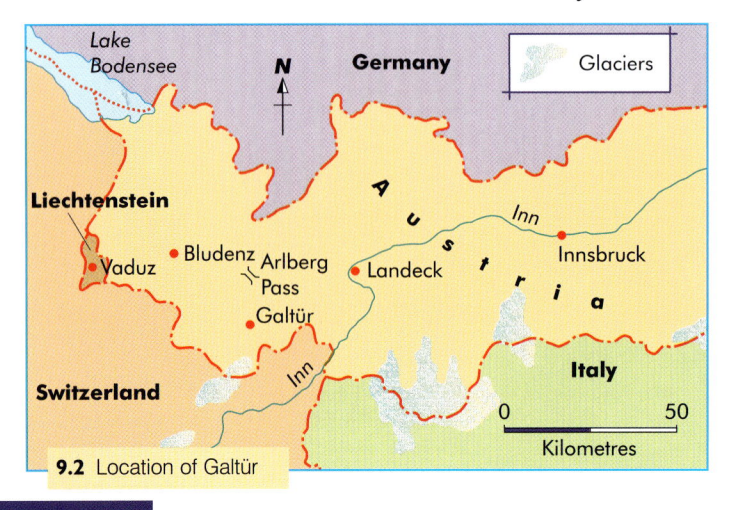

9.1 An avalanche

9.2 Location of Galtür

Tuesday 23 February 1999
A wall of snow, 5 m high, smashed through the centre of Galtür just after 4 pm. It crushed cars, hurling them across roads. Many houses were completely buried, and the snow and ice cleanly sliced off the top of one building. Snow was still falling heavily at night, with another 50 cm expected by the morning.

Wednesday 24 February
The avalanche which hit Galtür last night is reported to have killed at least 8 people, with up to 30 others missing. Residents managed to dig out alive about 20 people, although several of the survivors were said to be in a critical condition. Outside help could not at first reach the town as the main road had been blocked by an earlier avalanche, and bad weather prevented helicopters from flying in.

Thursday 25 February
The death toll from Tuesday's avalanche was put at 16, with 29 people still missing. Austrian television showed scores of rescuers using either long metal probes or specially trained sniffer dogs in an attempt to detect survivors buried under the masses of snow. A steady stream of helicopters took pallets of fresh fruit, vegetables and other foodstuffs into Galtür, returning with survivors and tourists. Estimates suggest that 2500 tourists had been helicoptered out of the town.

Saturday 27 February
Rescuers today recovered the body of a German girl believed to be the last of 38 people killed by Tuesday's avalanche. Roads to the town were open for the first time in over a week. Weather forecasters said the threat of further avalanches was diminishing as higher temperatures had reduced the amount of snow on mountainsides. Officials in Galtür claimed $20 million had been spent on avalanche protection structures. Local records showed that the town had been destroyed by an avalanche in 1689 when 250 people were killed.

9.3 The Galtür avalanche, as described in Internet reports

9.4 Galtür after the avalanche

9.5 Rescue operations in Galtür

Galtür The small alpine town of Galtür is situated in western Austria close to the border with Switzerland (**9.2**). The town and its 700 residents and an estimated 3000 tourists had been cut off by heavy snowfalls and avalanches for several days prior to Tuesday 23 February when its devastation was to become world news. Figure **9.3** summarises several reports, taken from the Internet, which describe the events of that afternoon and several subsequent days.

Galtür is situated 200 m from the base of the mountains. As it had never been affected by an avalanche in 600 years, it was considered so safe that even snow fences had not been erected (**9.6**). Indeed, computer-simulated tests showed that even an extreme 1 in 150-year avalanche would not reach the settlement. Even so, three 'building zones' did exist:
- a red zone where no buildings were allowed
- a yellow zone where all buildings had to be reinforced to withstand avalanches
- a green zone where there were no building restrictions.

Six months of scientific investigation after the event discovered several previously unknown processes at work within avalanches, and that this particular avalanche was 100 m in height and travelled at 300 km/hr.

Avalanche prediction and management

There is a close link between avalanches and:
- the time of year – almost 80 per cent occur between January and March
- altitude – over 80 per cent occur between 1500 and 3000 m
- favoured 'tracks' down which avalanches travel.

Although it is possible to predict *when* and *in which regions* avalanches are most likely to occur, it is less easy to predict exactly *where* the event will happen. It is this unpredictability that makes them a major hazard in alpine areas such as western Austria. However, despite this uncertainty, it is possible to protect life and property to a certain extent, by setting up advance warning systems, training rescue teams and taking measures such as those shown in **9.6**.

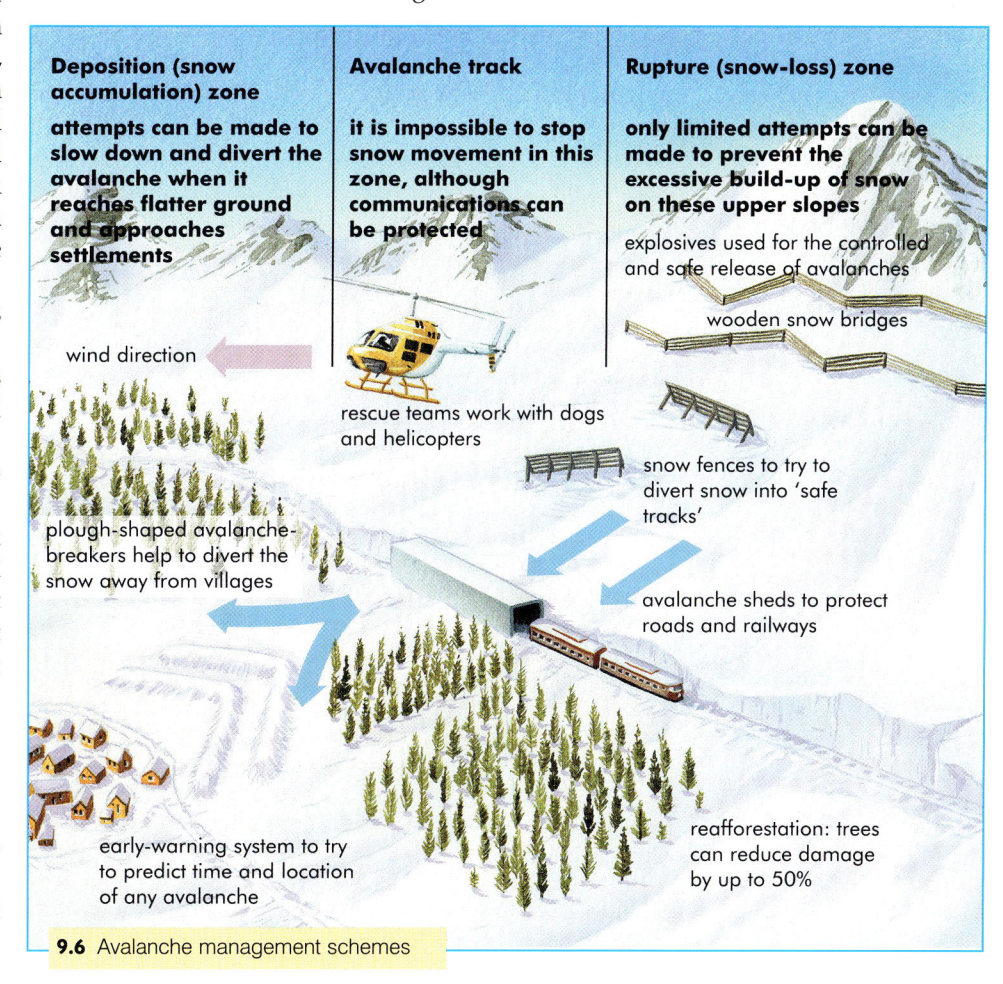

Deposition (snow accumulation) zone
attempts can be made to slow down and divert the avalanche when it reaches flatter ground and approaches settlements

wind direction

plough-shaped avalanche-breakers help to divert the snow away from villages

early-warning system to try to predict time and location of any avalanche

Avalanche track
it is impossible to stop snow movement in this zone, although communications can be protected

rescue teams work with dogs and helicopters

Rupture (snow-loss) zone
only limited attempts can be made to prevent the excessive build-up of snow on these upper slopes

explosives used for the controlled and safe release of avalanches

wooden snow bridges

snow fences to try to divert snow into 'safe tracks'

avalanche sheds to protect roads and railways

reafforestation: trees can reduce damage by up to 50%

9.6 Avalanche management schemes

Southern Italy – earthquakes

Italy is the most seismically active of all European countries. Although its volcanoes are major tourist attractions and its volcanic rocks give geothermal power and provide building materials, frequent earthquakes and earth movements throughout historic times have proved devastating to both human life and property.

Italy is located where two small crustal plates, the Messina and the Adriatic, are sandwiched between two large plates, the African and the Eurasian (9.7). The African plate (which consists of continental crust) is moving slowly northwards towards the Eurasian Plate (also continental crust).

1 The African plate is pushing the oceanic crust of the Messina plate downwards to form a destructive plate boundary (9.8). This means that:
   a the resultant increase in pressure can trigger severe earthquakes, e.g. Messina (83 000 deaths in 1908) and Catania (150 000 deaths in 1963) – both in Sicily.
   b the crust melts, partly due to heat resulting from friction caused by contact with the Eurasian plate and partly due to the increase in heat as it re-enters the mantle, to give volcanic activity, e.g. Etna and Vesuvius.
2 The African plate is pushing the Adriatic plate upwards to form a collision plate boundary. This has resulted in the formation of the Apennines and, again, the triggering of severe earthquakes, e.g. Gemona (where over 1000 people died in 1976), Balvano (3000 deaths and 18 000 made homeless in 1980), and Assisi (1997).

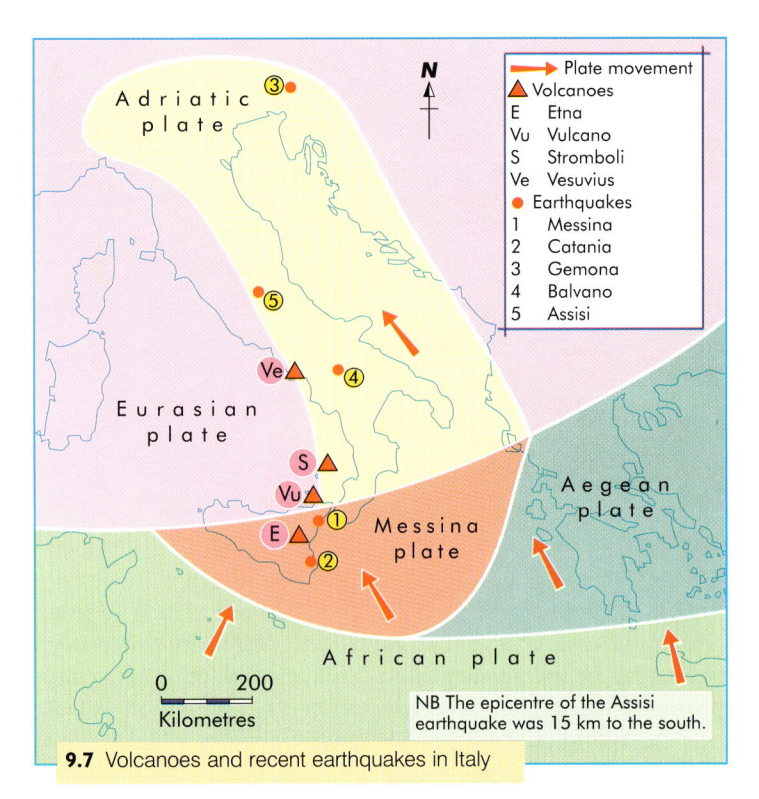

9.7 Volcanoes and recent earthquakes in Italy

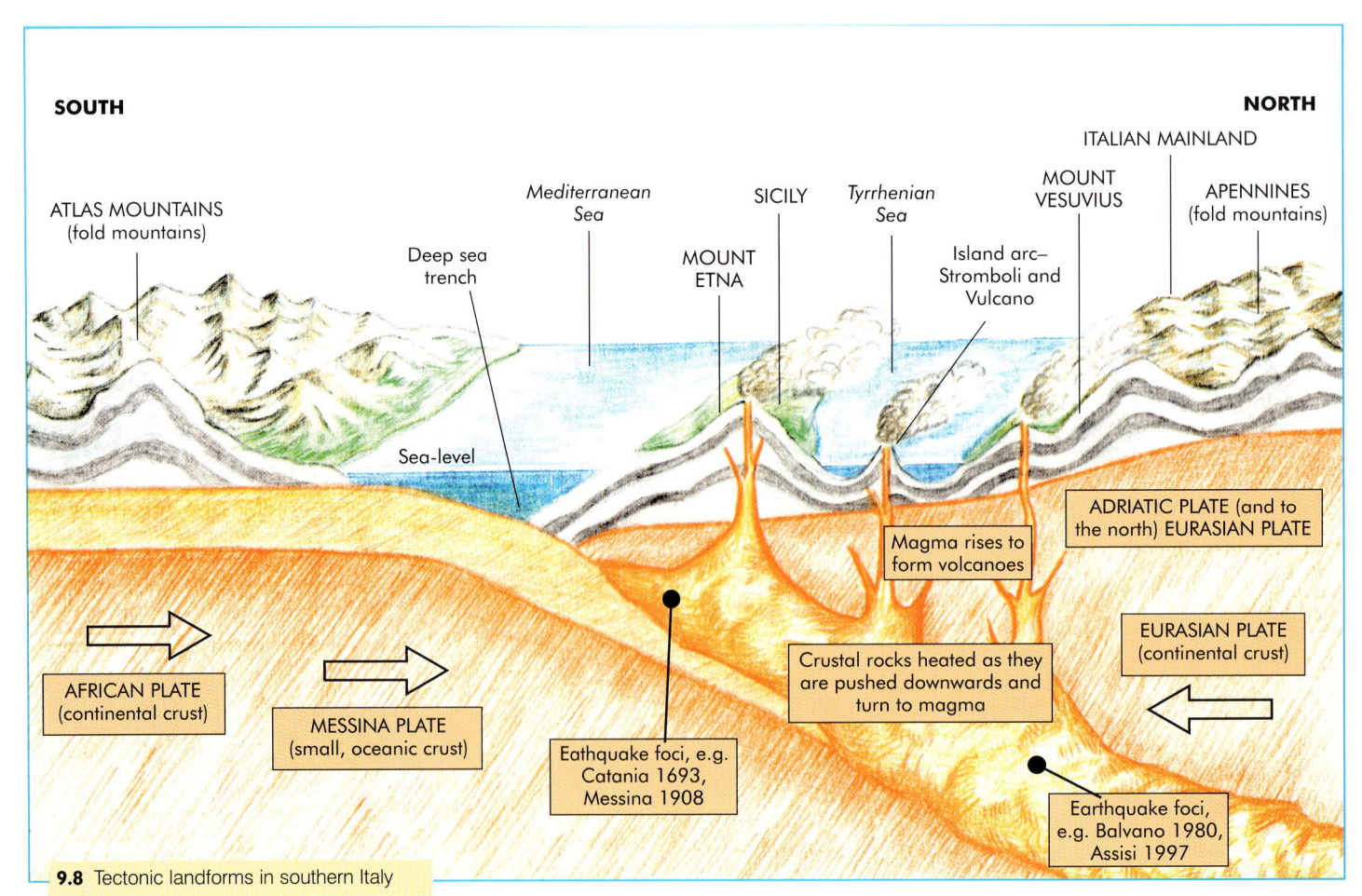

Legend:
- → Plate movement
- △ Volcanoes
- E Etna
- Vu Vulcano
- S Stromboli
- Ve Vesuvius
- ● Earthquakes
- 1 Messina
- 2 Catania
- 3 Gemona
- 4 Balvano
- 5 Assisi

NB The epicentre of the Assisi earthquake was 15 km to the south.

9.8 Tectonic landforms in southern Italy

9.9 The Basilica of St Francis of Assisi

Assisi (Umbria)

Assisi is one of many hilltop towns in central Italy. It is best known as the birthplace of St Francis (1182), the patron saint of animals and the founder of the Franciscan monastic order. During his lifetime, two churches (the Upper and Lower Basilicas) were built in the town (**9.9**) and later his life was recorded, in the Upper Basilica, in a famous series of 28 frescos (wall paintings) accredited to Giotto (1296), one of the earliest of the Renaissance painters.

Assisi experienced major earthquakes in 1832, 1854, 1915 and 1982. The 1982 event, the 18th to affect the region since 1700, caused minor damage to the Upper Basilicata. This was nothing, however, compared with the earthquake of 19 September 1997. The first warning earthquake came in the early hours and caused people to move from their homes to the comparative safety of the streets. In mid-morning, a second earthquake, measuring 5.7 on the Richter scale, caused considerable damage (especially to the Upper Basilica – **9.10**) and some loss of life (**9.11**). This was followed by strong aftershocks, one measuring 4.9, that were still being experienced two weeks after the event (**9.11**).

9.10 Inside the damaged Basilica

The day after the event

In Assisi, six people were killed (five more in the surrounding area) and 80 per cent of the buildings damaged. Part of the roof of the 13th-century Upper Basilica of St Francis collapsed during the second earthquake. Two Franciscan monks and two surveyors who were in the Basilica assessing damage caused by the first 'quake, were killed by falling masonry, and it was thought that many of the frescos had been seriously damaged. The nearby 12th-century cathedral has been made unstable and most private dwellings are damaged.

Three weeks after the event

Strong aftershocks, one measuring 4.9, were still being experienced in the region. Each major tremor caused panic among the townspeople who were afraid to return home and were sleeping in tents and public buildings. Several of the shockwaves caused further damage to the Basilica and other buildings.

One week after the event

Reports suggest that most of Giotto's 28 frescos appear to have survived, although restorers will have a mammoth task in piecing together the thousands of fragments strewn across the damaged building. The tomb of St Francis, under the Lower Basilica, was said to be safe. However, recriminations have already begun. Some 30 years ago, wooden beams and joints that had supported the Basilica for over 700 years and had withstood several earthquakes had been replaced by reinforced concrete. The mayor's attempts to close the town to tourists failed when business people objected (80 per cent of Assisi's income comes from tourism). Up to 13 000 people, many elderly, were still spending the chilly nights in temporary shelters, complaining that the world seemed more interested in the damaged frescos than with homeless people.

9.11 Newspaper accounts of the aftermath of the Assisi earthquake

Merapi – a volcano in Indonesia

Indonesia lies on a destructive plate boundary. It is part of an island arc (the country consists of over 13 000 islands) formed where oceanic crust is forced downwards under continental crust. As the oceanic crust melts, partly due to heat caused by friction with the continental crust and partly due to the increase in temperature as it enters the mantle, some of the newly formed magma rises to the surface to form volcanoes. Indonesia, with a total of 130, has one-third of the world's active volcanoes. Of these, 34 are located on the island of Java, including Merapi ('Mountain of Fire') which is the most active (**9.12**). Merapi, which is considered sacred, has killed people on 10 occasions since 1920 and caused villages on its flanks to be evacuated even more frequently (**9.13**).

Year	No. people killed	Houses destroyed
1930 (e)	1369	1109
1954 (e)	64	144
1956 (e)	–	2
1961 (e)	5	109
1969 (e)	3	91
1969 (m)	3	231
1974 (m)	9	29
1975 (m)	–	214
1976 (m)	27	385
1984 (e)	–	–
1986 (m)	1	–
1994 (e)	61	25
2000 (e)	–	56

(e) = eruption   (m) = mudflow

9.13 Effects of recent eruptions

9.12 Merapi volcano

The 1994 eruption

When Merapi erupted in November 1994, it destroyed several villages and killed over 60 people – a large number for a volcanic event. Worst-hit was Turgo, a village 6 km away. Villagers claimed that the eruption was both sudden and violent. Before they had a chance to escape, the area was covered in a thick cloud of red-hot ash that made it too dark for them to see anything (**9.14**). The ash caused houses to collapse, and villagers working in the fields were badly burnt where their skin was exposed. As the cloud dispersed, survivors fled with their few remaining possessions to temporary shelters that are provided in anticipation of such an event (**9.15**).

The ejection of materials such as ash, rocks and gases at the time of an eruption, is said to be a primary hazard. In many instances, however, this may be followed by later, or secondary, hazards. Around Merapi, the secondary hazard is lahars (**9.16**). Lahars are caused when the heavy monsoon rains pick up ash and other volcanic material, and the resultant mudflow rushes downhill covering settlements and farmland (compare Pinatubo in the Philippines in 1991).

9.14 Cloud of red-hot ash

9.15 People fleeing the eruption

9.16 A lahar (mudflow)

9.17 Fertile soil and a hot, wet climate give high crop yields

Why do people live around the volcano?
Although people know that living near to the Merapi volcano is dangerous, they perceive the risk to be worth taking. This is because material ejected from the volcano rapidly breaks down (weathers) into a fertile soil that is rich in the minerals required for plant growth. The productive soil, which gives high crop yields, has encouraged intensive farming. Added to this, the climate, which is consistently hot and wet, allows farmers to grow three crops a year (**9.17**). The main crops are rice, grown mainly for their own use, and fruit and vegetables, which are cash crops for sale in urban markets such as Jakarta or for export overseas.

However, high yields have led to a high population density and a shortage of available farmland. This means that, after an eruption, farmers in the Merapi region have little choice but to return to their villages and to rebuild their homes.

Responses to the Merapi hazard
These include predicting and giving advance warning of future eruptions, protecting people who live in high-risk areas, educating villagers in evacuation procedures, and resettling people in lower-risk areas. These are summarised in **9.18**.

Prediction – monitoring future eruptions
Volcanic activity in the Merapi volcano is monitored using seismometers. The equipment at individual sites is fairly simple. In one method, smoke created by the burning of kerosene produces a layer of carbon on a roll of paper. The roll of paper, which is turned slowly by a car battery, passes under a recording needle. Should there be any earth movement, the needle jumps and the tremor is recorded. Data from individual stations is collected and recorded centrally. Also, each month a team visits the summit to note any changes in pressure and temperature. Hopefully, this should enable scientists to give villagers sufficient time to seek safety before an eruption occurs.

Protection – mudflow dams
Dams have been built down each valley leading from Merapi to hold back lahars (mudflows). The dams trap the mud, which can later be spread over fields, and slowly release the water. Over 70 dams have been built to protect villages, roads, a major canal system and tourist sites.

Evacuation
A taskforce of local people has been specifically trained to give emergency treatment to the injured and to organise transport to evacuation camps and temporary accommodation.

Resettlement
Settlement is not allowed in a Prohibited Area near to the summit of the volcano, although farming is allowed there. Villagers, evacuated either from the Prohibited Area or from their village, are given two options:

1. They can live in relocation settlements where concrete houses are safer and have electricity, but where there is no land to farm.
2. They can move (a process of transmigration introduced by the government) to less crowded islands such as Sumatra.

In reality very few people elect to move, and most return to their villages however high the volcanic risk.

9.18 Responses to the Merapi hazard

Hong Kong – typhoons

Typhoons (the Cantonese word for 'big wind') are tropical revolving storms characterised by intense low pressure, hurricane-force winds and torrential rainfall. They occur in the China Sea region, especially between May and December. Typhoons, like their hurricane counterparts in the Americas, can cause widespread damage and loss of life.

Hong Kong is well acquainted with these storms, and fully equipped to handle the situation. There are various advance warning signals posted at entrances to MTR (mass transit railway) stations and on public buildings (9.19). The signals start with No.1, meaning standby, and progress to No.10, indicating a serious typhoon centred over the area (9.20). Signal No.1 aims to give people two days' warning of a typhoon event and time for ships to seek shelter in the specially constructed typhoon shelters (9.21). The Royal Observatory also give warnings of other hazards likely to be created by a typhoon together with how and where to obtain up-to-date information on a passing storm (9.22).

9.19 No.1 typhoon signal on Victoria Peak

9.21 New typhoon shelter, Kowloon Harbour

Signal (four categories of tropical cyclone based on wind speed)		Meaning of the signal	What you should do Specific advice is contained in weather broadcasts, but the following general precautions can be taken
Standby	1	A tropical cyclone is centred within about 800 km of Hong Kong and may later affect Hong Kong. Hong Kong is placed in a state of alert because the tropical cyclone is a potential threat and may cause destructive winds later.	**Listen to weather broadcasts.** Some preliminary precautions are desirable and you should take the existence of the tropical cyclone into account in planning your activities.
Strong wind A Tropical depression	3	Strong wind expected or blowing, with a sustained speed of 41–62 km/hr and gusts that may exceed 110 km/hr. The timing of the hoisting of the signal is aimed to give about 12 hours' advance warning of a strong wind in Victoria Harbour but the warning period may be shorter for more exposed waters.	**Take all necessary precautions.** Secure all loose objects, particularly on balconies and rooftops. Secure hoardings, scaffolding and temporary structures. Clear gutters and drains. Take full precautions for the safety of boats. Ships in port normally leave for typhoon anchorages or buoys. Ferry services may soon be affected by wind or waves. Even at this stage heavy rain accompanied by violent squalls may occur.
Gale or storm B Tropical storm	8	Gale or storm expected or blowing, with a sustained wind speed of 63–117 km/hr from the quarter indicated and gusts that may exceed 180 km/hr. The timing of the replacement of the Strong Wind Signal No.3 by the appropriate one of these four signals, is aimed to give about 12 hours' advance warning of a gale in Victoria Harbour, but the sustained wind speed may reach 63 km/hr within a shorter period over more exposed waters. Expected changes in the direction of the wind will be indicated by corresponding changes of these signals.	**Complete all precautions as soon as possible.** It is extremely dangerous to delay precautions until the hoisting of No.9 or No.10 signals as these are signals of great urgency. Windows and doors should be bolted and shuttered. Stay indoors when the winds increase to avoid flying debris, but if you must go out, keep well clear of overhead wires and hoardings. All schools and law courts close and ferries will probably stop running at short notice. The sea-level will probably be higher than normal, particularly in narrow inlets. If this happens near the time of normal high tide then low-lying areas may have to be evacuated very quickly. Heavy rain may cause flooding, rockfalls and mudslips.
Increasing gale or storm C Severe tropical storm	9	Gale or storm expected to increase significantly in strength. This signal will be hoisted when the sustained wind speed is expected to increase and come within the range 88–117 km/hr during the next few hours.	**Stay where you are** if you are reasonably protected and away from exposed windows and doors. This signal implies that the centre of a severe tropical storm or a typhoon will come close to Hong Kong. If the eye passes over there will be a lull lasting from a few minutes to some hours, but be prepared for a sudden resumption of destructive winds from a different direction.
Hurricane D Typhoon	10	Hurricane-force winds expected or blowing, with a sustained wind speed reaching upwards from 118 km/hr and with gusts that may exceed 220 km/hr.	

9.20 Typhoon warning signals, Hong Kong

Issued by the Royal Observatory © Hong Kong Crown Copyright 1986

The **Standby Signal** is an advisory signal indicating the possibility of destructive winds occurring in Hong Kong. It is important to realise that whilst the **Tropical Cyclone Warning Signals** give warnings of winds expected or blowing near sea-level over open water and similarly exposed areas, they do not specifically warn of other dangers which may result from the tropical cyclone. These include flooding in low-lying areas as a result of a storm surge which may cause the sea-level to rise considerably higher than is normal, and the destructive effects of very heavy rain which usually accompanies tropical cyclones. This rain can cause flooding, landslips and ground subsidence. Small streams can turn into raging torrents within a short period, bringing danger to anyone in their vicinity. Rocks may be dislodged from hillsides and there may be mudslips. It is therefore important that you should listen to broadcast weather bulletins to obtain information on all expected adverse weather so that you make take appropriate precautions against violent winds, heavy rain and storm surges. **SIMPLY KNOWING WHAT SIGNAL IS DISPLAYED IS NOT ENOUGH.** Tropical cyclone warning bulletins are broadcast at two minutes to and half-past every hour when any of the signals No.8 to No.10 is displayed. If you do not have a radio or if you miss a broadcast bulletin, information on the signal status of the tropical cyclone may be obtained from the Public Enquiry Service Centre of the City and New Territories Administration Headquarters. Tel. 3-692255. Please do not telephone the Royal Observatory because the telephone lines there must be kept free for the dissemination of warnings and other urgent operational requirements.

Royal Observatory, Hong Kong

9.22 Possible hazards resulting from a typhoon

9.23 Consequences of a landslip in Hong Kong

Typhoon York was a particularly damaging storm that passed over Hong Kong in September 1999. Weather details and newspaper reports of the event are given in **9.24**.

Tropical cyclone signal no./category	Time of hoisting	Date	Other warnings
No.1	1045	Mon 13th	
No.3 (tropical depression)	1015	Wed 15th	
No.8 (NW storm)	0315	Thurs 16th	
No.9 (severe tropical storm)	0520	"	
No.10* (typhoon)	0645	"	Landslip warning
No.8 (SW storm)	1745	"	Flood warning
No.3	2210	"	
No.3 lowered	0045	Fri 17th	

* No.10 hoisted for 11 hours – the longest time ever recorded
NB Eye of typhoon passed shortly after midday on Thurs 16th.

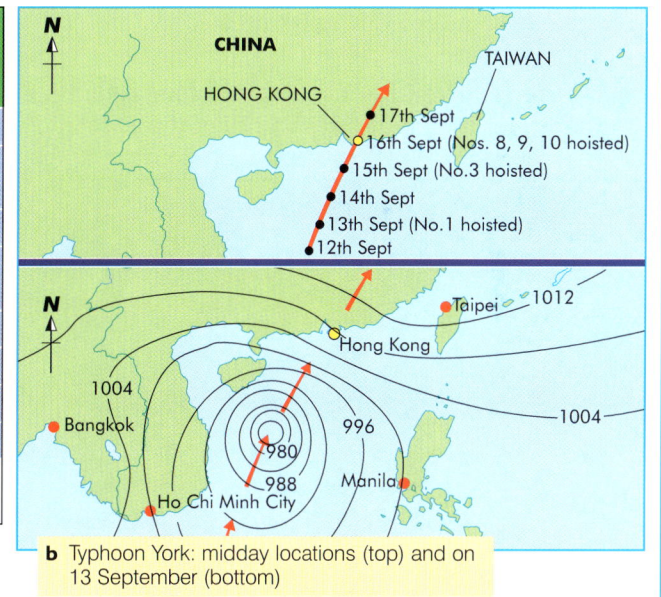

a Typhoon York, 13–17 September 1999

b Typhoon York: midday locations (top) and on 13 September (bottom)

1 Situation at 1800 hours on Thursday 16 September
More than 500 people are in emergency shelters. There has been 1 death (caused by flying debris), 200 reported injuries and 40 roads closed by landslides or debris [**9.23**]. All public transport on land and sea has been suspended, except for the underground portions of the MTR, and all schools have, and will remain, closed.

2 Situation at 1800 hours on Saturday 18 September
Typhoon York killed 3 people, including a surfer swept away by high seas. Initial estimates put the total bill at tens of billions of dollars. CLP Power say that 1700 homes are still without electricity, although supplies have been restored to 12 300. Work has begun to clear an estimated 4300 uprooted trees. Initial checks on three high-rise office blocks in downtown Hong Kong found 429 damaged windows, mainly at the Revenue and Immigration Towers. The storm grounded all planes for 24 hours and forced the cancellation of 468 flights from Chek Lap Kok International Airport, but the airport re-opened at 1500 hours yesterday. It took 200 extra flights to help clear the massive backlog of passengers.

c Reports given in the *South China Morning Post*

9.24 Accounts of Typhoon York, September 1999

10 River flooding and management

The rivers Severn and Wye (UK) – the flood hazard in the UK

Flood defence schemes reduce the risk of flooding and protect those who live near rivers and the sea. Although there are 36 000 km of flood defences in England and Wales that give a high level of protection, they cannot be guaranteed to eliminate the risk of flooding. It is the role of the Environment Agency (EA) to issue flood warnings to people so that they can take action to protect themselves and their property. Flood prediction is not, however, an exact science and no flood warning system can cover every eventuality, even though the EA uses the latest technology to monitor rainfall, river levels, tides and sea conditions. When the EA anticipates that there is a risk of flooding, it issues warnings to the police, local authorities and the media and, where local agreements have been made, directly to those most likely to be affected.

Flood warnings given by the EA are colour coded – each colour indicates the predicted severity of the event.

Yellow warning – flooding likely to affect low-lying farmland and roads near to rivers.
Amber warning – flooding likely to affect isolated properties, roads and large areas of farmland near to rivers.
Red warning – serious flooding likely to affect many properties, roads and large areas of farmland, causing major disruption to everyday life.

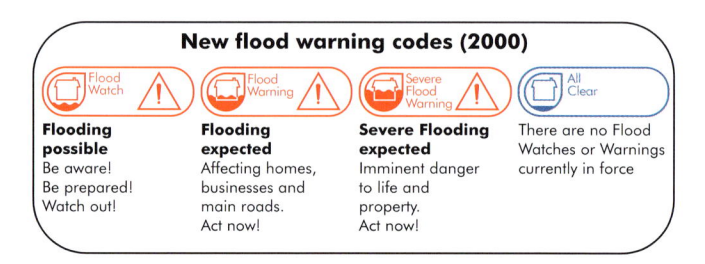

New flood warning codes (2000)

Flood Watch	Flood Warning	Severe Flood Warning	All Clear
Flooding possible Be aware! Be prepared! Watch out!	**Flooding expected** Affecting homes, businesses and main roads. Act now!	**Severe Flooding expected** Imminent danger to life and property. Act now!	There are no Flood Watches or Warnings currently in force

While it is the task of the EA to issue flood warnings, others are involved too:
- The police co-ordinate the response to major emergencies and, along with the fire and rescue service, supervise the evacuation of properties.
- Local authorities produce contingency plans for civil emergencies and deal with some aspects of flood control management, e.g. the provision of sandbags and emergency shelters.

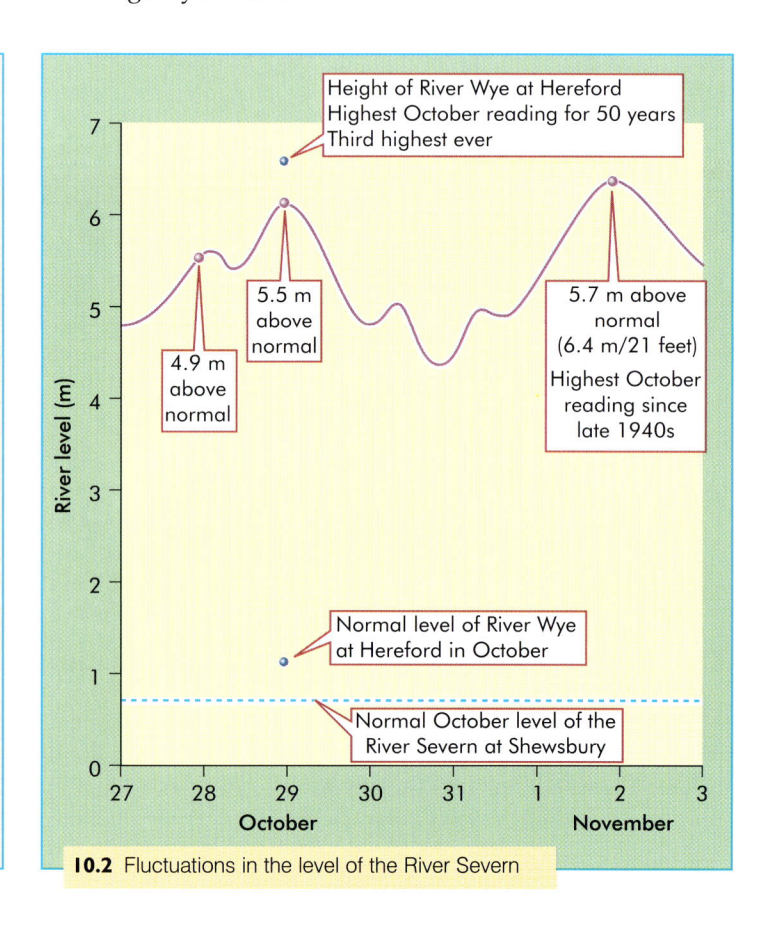

10.1 Flood warnings, 29 October 1998

10.2 Fluctuations in the level of the River Severn

29 October (Thursday), 1998

Following a week of severe weather which claimed the lives of 12 people across Britain, red flood warnings are in force for a 160 km stretch of the River Severn from Welshpool to Worcester (10.1). The EA describes the flooding as 'critical' and the Met Office is predicting more bad weather for the night ahead. Shrewsbury is expecting some of its worst flooding of the century. Three RNLI lifeboat crews have already been sent to Herefordshire. Several places are bracing themselves for a repeat of the Easter floods which were the worst in the area for 150 years.

30 October

Forecasters are predicting more heavy rain over the coming weekend. All road crossings of the Wye in Hereford and of the Severn in Shrewsbury are closed (10.3), with the exception of one toll bridge. With so many red alert warnings, several councils have set up emergency centres in schools and community centres. Two flood peaks are moving down the Severn (10.2). The first, which reached Shrewsbury two days ago and Worcester yesterday, is expected at Tewkesbury this afternoon and at Gloucester tonight. The second peak, a day behind the first, gave the highest October level at Shrewsbury since recordings began in 1672.

31 October

Police are warning people living near to stretches of the Rivers Severn and Wye to stand by for evacuation because of the threat of further severe flooding following more heavy rain. The EA has appealed to sightseers to avoid the area for their own safety. At places like Bewdley local people are struggling with some of the worst flooding since the late 1940s (10.4). The EA says that while river levels are beginning to fall, in view of the Met Office's predicted 25 mm of rain, the situation remains critical.

2 November

Although the Severn is falling at Shrewsbury, it remains 10 times its normal level at Bewdley for this time of year. The Met Office has issued a warning of further flooding after predicting another period of persistent heavy rain.

3 November

A massive clean-up operation is underway despite showers and strong winds. Residents of Bewdley are clearing away mud left by the receding waters despite the warning that it may have been contaminated with untreated sewage. Meanwhile experts are saying that changes in the global climate mean that Britain can expect more of this extreme weather.

In 2000, in exactly the same week as in 1998, equally severe flooding again affected the Severn Valley, especially at Shrewsbury, Bewdley and Worcester. At the same time, flooding was experienced as far afield as Sussex (second time in three weeks), North Yorkshire (the Ouse at York reached its highest level in over 100 years), along the Yorkshire Derwent (second time in 20 months), and in Somerset and North Wales. With, at times, over 35 rivers having severe flood warnings posted, the floods were described as 'the greatest in extent since 1947 and in some places as severe'.

10.3 Shrewsbury surrounded by the swollen River Severn

10.4 Floodwaters in Bewdley, Worcestershire

Bangladesh – the river flood of 1998

Flooding is an annual event in Bangladesh. The monsoon rains cause rivers such as the Jamuna (Brahmaputra) and Padma (Ganges) to overflow their banks between July and mid-August (**10.5**). Most of Bangladesh's 125 million inhabitants live on the floodplains of these rivers (**10.6**). For most of them, the seasonal flood is essential for their survival as it brings water in which to grow the main crops of rice and jute as well as silt to fertilise their fields. Flooding of 20 per cent of the country is considered beneficial for crops and the ecological balance. However, a figure much less than that can result in food shortages, while an inundation much in excess can cause considerable loss of life, ruin crops and seriously damage property (**10.7**). In 1998, 68 per cent of the country was flooded, some places for over 70 days. This flood was unprecedented in terms of both its magnitude and duration. Apart from destroying crops and basic infrastructural features such as roads and bridges, it caused the deaths of 918 people and made more than 20 million homeless (**10.8**).

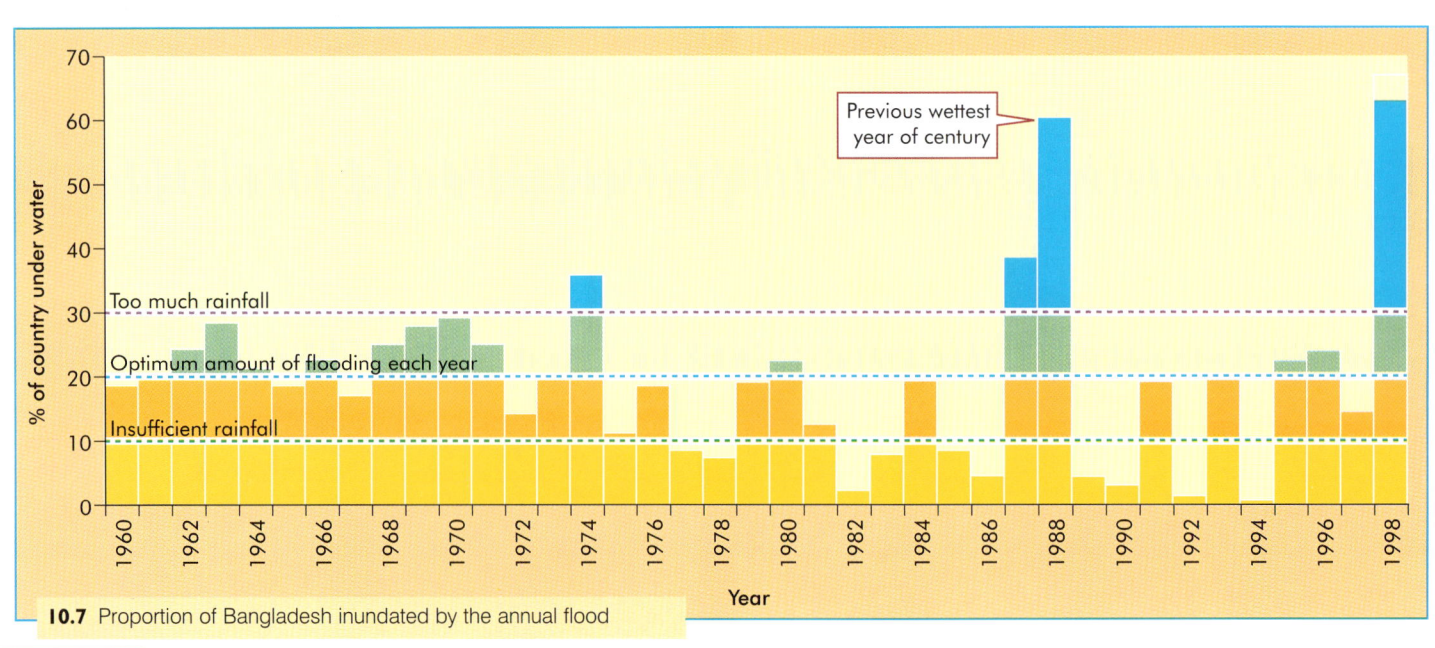

10.6 Floodwaters covering low-lying areas of the country

10.5 Major rivers in Bangladesh

10.7 Proportion of Bangladesh inundated by the annual flood

10.8 Effect of the 1998 flood

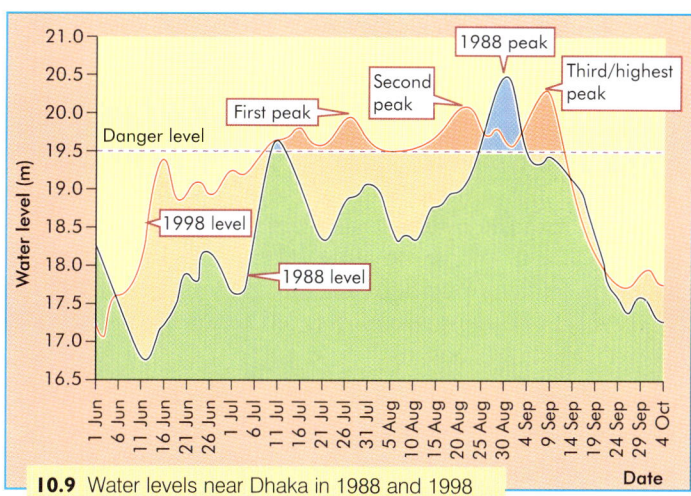

10.9 Water levels near Dhaka in 1988 and 1998

Rice (1.35 million tonnes)	US$ 250.5m
Wheat (27 000 tonnes)	US$ 5.5m
Seeds and fertiliser	US$ 31.7m
Tube-wells (sanitation)	US$ 9.4m
Medicine and equipment	US$ 1.8m
Veterinary medicine	US$ 5.0m
Repairs to embankments	US$ 150.0m
Urban road repairs	US$ 16.5m
Bridge repairs	US$ 34.2m
Primary school repairs	US$ 95.7m
Re-equipping health centres	US$ 4.5m
Rural road repairs	US$ 53.4m

NB Bangladesh's normal annual food deficit is about 2.1 million metric tonnes. The estimated food loss in 1998 is 2.2 million metric tonnes. The resultant food shortage for this year is expected to be 4.3 million metric tonnes.

10.10 Urgent aid requirements, August 1998

May and June There was very little rainfall in the catchment area, 92 per cent of which lies beyond the national borders of Bangladesh.

July Heavy rain at the beginning of the month caused the Brahmaputra, Meghna and Ganges rivers to rise rapidly. When the river reached a peak on the 28th (**10.9**), 30 per cent of Bangladesh was under water.

August The flood situation slowly improved until the 20th when most rivers again exceeded their danger levels. A second flood peak, reached on the 30th, saw floodwater covering 41 per cent of the country.

September Further heavy rain caused the rivers to reach a third peak – the highest – on the 7th. By this time, 68 per cent of the country was, or had been, under water. Although the situation improved after that date, it was the end of the month before the floodwaters drained away from many areas.

Requirements for immediate relief
Urgent requirements were requested on 26 August – two weeks before the third flood peak and a month before the floodwaters finally receded (**10.10**).

Causes of river flooding
- Much of Bangladesh consists of the floodplain and delta of the rivers Ganges and Brahmaputra. Over half the country lies below 6 m above sea-level. Once the rivers overflow their banks or breach the protective floodbanks (levées), the water can spread over vast distances, inundating roads, railways, farmland and settlements.
- Bangladesh has a monsoon climate. This means that, although most places receive between 1800 and 2600 mm of rain a year (the average for London is about 600 mm), over 80 per cent of that total is concentrated in four or five months (June to September).
- The period of heavy rain coincides with that of the highest temperatures. The high temperatures melt ice and snow in the Himalayas where the Ganges, Brahmaputra and their tributaries have their headwaters.
- Spring tides (they occur monthly) and/or tropical cyclones (most frequent in summer and autumn – pages 68 and 69) affect the Bay of Bengal and prevent floodwater from the rivers draining into the sea.
- Global warming is causing (i) glaciers in the Himalayas to melt (increasing runoff) and (ii) sea-level in the Bay of Bengal to rise.
- An earthquake in Assam in 1950 caused a rapid increase in the amount of silt in the Brahmaputra. This silt has since been deposited within the channel of the river, increasing the flood risk.
- Human mismanagement has increased the magnitude and frequency of flooding by (i) building upon the floodplains (the process of urbanisation) and (ii) cutting down trees in upper catchment areas such as Nepal (deforestation increases the rate and amount of runoff).

The Yangtze (China) – river flooding: natural and human

The Yangtze rises on the Tibetan Plateau and flows 6380 km before entering the East China Sea just north of Shanghai. Although it has always been prone to flooding, both the frequency and the intensity have increased in recent years (10.11). During the same time, there has been a rapid growth in both population size and in human activity on the river's floodplain, which has led to an increase in the adverse effects of flooding.

Flooding in the 20th century

1931 – 140 000 deaths and up to 40 million made homeless.
1954 – 33 000 deaths.
1981 and 1991 – large areas inundated.
1995 – 1300 deaths and up to 100 million made homeless.
1998 – worst flood for over half a century with the river, in places, reaching its highest ever level – a level that was maintained for over two months (10.12). There were an estimated 3000 deaths, 5.6 million homes washed away, 30 million made homeless, and huge areas of crops destroyed. The river rose steadily during June, and by early July 100 000 soldiers and police were working in teams, 24 hours a day and 7 days a week, strengthening floodbanks (levées) around Wuhan (a city east of the Three Gorges). On 21 July, 280 mm of rain fell on Wuhan (about half of London's annual total) and the next day the city experienced the first of several flood peaks that it was to experience over the next two months. Later, and by the time that several smaller cities had been submerged for over a month, the Chinese authorities admitted they were allowing smaller settlements to flood in order to protect larger cities. As one official claimed, 'by diverting the Yangtze, some villages were destroyed but the very real threat to Wuhan's seven million residents was averted'.

Causes of flooding

- Large areas of the Yangtze basin receive high annual amounts of rainfall. Most of the rain is seasonal, falling in intensive storms associated with the summer monsoon (pages 5 and 73).
- The rains arrive as temperatures across China rise. One result of this is the rapid melting of snow and glaciers in China's western mountains where the Yangtze has its source.
- Large areas of the upper basin were deforested in the 1950s and 1960s during Chairman Mao's so-called 'Great Leap Forward'. Estimates suggest that one-third of the basin was cleared between then and 1988 (pages 90 and 91). Deforestation reduced interception and increased runoff and soil erosion – the latter causing the bed of the Yangtze to rise even higher above its floodplain downriver near Wuhan.

10.11 The Yangtze flood, 1998

10.12 Fluctuating seasonal levels of the Yangtze

- The building of houses, factories, roads and railways on the floodplain has reduced the area of land that once could safely be allowed to flood.

Flooding between 2003 and 2007

The Chinese have been convinced for several decades that the only way to control the Yangtze and to reduce its flood risk was to build a dam across the river. This dam is now being built, against the advice of most people outside of China and a minority within China, at Sandouping where the Yangtze leaves its scenic Three Gorges section (pages 92 and 93). The dam, which is part of the Three Gorges Project, is 1983 m long and 185 m high (**10.13**). It is expected to begin holding back floodwater from 2003 onwards, although it will be between 2007 and 2009 before the project is completed.

One, if not the main, benefit of the dam will be its ability to store water from a flood whose magnitude is not expected to occur more frequently than once in every 100 years (the previous biggest flood before that of 1998 was in 1881). Those in favour of the dam argue that as the river's discharge can be controlled and the floodwater released gradually, then up to 100 million people living in places downriver will be safe. Opponents of the project point out that once the scheme is completed, a lake 600 km long will have formed behind the dam. As the level of the lake rises it will submerge numerous settlements along its sides, forcing 1.3 million people to move home (**10.14** shows the predicted water levels in 2003 and 2009). Figure **10.15** shows the large town of Fengdu, which will be totally submerged (refer again to **10.12**). Figure **10.16** shows a new settlement being built at the eventual level of the lake. In other words, to reduce the flood risk in one part of the Yangtze basin, other places are being permanently flooded. The great unknown is what happens if a 1 in 1000 year flood occurs or if an earthquake, bad dam construction or the sheer weight of water in the lake causes the dam to collapse (pages 92 and 93).

10.13 The Three Gorges Dam under construction, 1999

10.14 Predicted lake levels in 2003 (135 m above sea-level) and 2007 (170 m above sea-level)

10.15 Fengdu (1999), which will be totally submerged

10.16 New settlement at the eventual level of the lake

11 Climatic issues

El Niño and La Niña – climatic change

The oceans store huge amounts of heat which enables them to influence the world's climate. If ocean temperatures change, this has a considerable effect on the weather of places on adjacent landmasses. The interaction between the ocean and the atmosphere has become a major scientific study – especially over the Pacific Ocean where the normal interrelationship (**11.1**) is periodically interrupted by what are now known as El Niño (**11.2**) and La Niña (**11.3**) events.

NORMAL CONDITIONS The usual circulation of air in the atmosphere (**11.1**) means:
- Air over the western Pacific (the Philippines, Indonesia and northern Australia) rises to give an area of low pressure. As the warm, moist air rises, it cools to give heavy rainfall.
- Air over the eastern Pacific (Central and South America) descends to give an area of high pressure. As the air descends it warms to give dry weather (the Atacama and Mexican deserts).
- Strong surface winds (the trade winds) blow from east (high pressure) to west (low pressure).
- The trade winds push surface water westwards – this is the equatorial current (sea-level is 60 cm higher in South-east Asia than it is in the Americas). The surface water is warmed, usually to over 28°C, by heat from the sun.
- As water is pushed away from South America, it is replaced by an upwelling of cold water. The colder water lowers temperatures, often to 20°C.

EL NIÑO An El Niño event occurs, on average, every three or four years and lasts for 12–18 months. It is called El Niño, which in Spanish means 'little child', because, in those years that it does occur, it appears shortly after Christmas. In contrast to normal conditions, there is a reversal in pressure, precipitation and, under extreme conditions, surface winds and ocean currents (**11.2**). This means:
- Air over the western Pacific now descends to give an area of high pressure. As the air descends it warms to give dry conditions and, under extreme conditions, drought (Australia in 1997). This can mean the late, or non-arrival, of the monsoon rains in South-east Asia.
- Air over the eastern Pacific rises to give an area of low pressure. As the air rises and cools, it gives uncharacteristically wet, and often stormy, weather. This can cause flooding in Peru and California (as during the strongest recorded El Niño event of 1997 and early 1998).
- The surface trade winds become very weak and may even change direction to blow from west (high pressure) to east (low pressure).
- The change in wind direction means that surface water is now pushed eastwards (so that sea-level is now higher off the American coast than in South-east Asia).
- The area of warm surface water now extends much further eastwards. The upwelling of cold water off the South American coast is reduced, allowing sea temperatures to rise by over 6°C.

LA NIÑA La Niña, which means 'little girl', gives climatic conditions that are the reverse of El Niño and an exaggeration of those experienced under normal conditions (**11.3**). A La Niña event often follows an El Niño event although its occurrence is less frequent and its effects less easy to predict. During a La Niña event:
- There is an increase in the uplift of warm, moist air over the western Pacific. This means that, compared with usual conditions, pressure falls even lower and rainfall totals and the frequency of tropical storms increase. (A La Niña event in 1998 was blamed for the worst ever floods in Bangladesh – pages 72–73).
- Pressure over the eastern Pacific becomes even higher, accentuating drought conditions in that part of the world.
- Due to the increase in pressure difference between the eastern and western Pacific, the strength of the surface trade winds, which blow from east to west, increases.
- The stronger trade winds push a greater volume of water westwards to give even higher sea-levels in the Philippines and Indonesia.
- With a greater volume of water pushed westwards, there is an increase in the upwelling of cold water off the South American coast. This lowers coastal temperatures by several degrees.

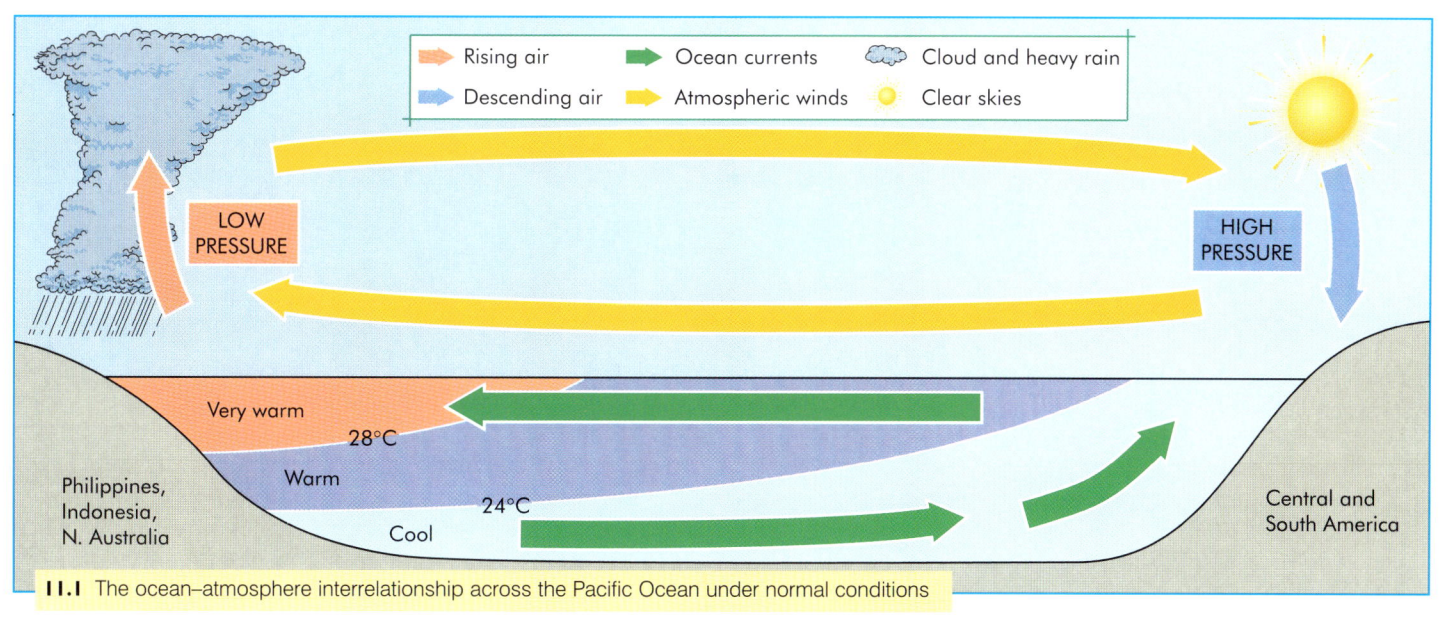

Legend:
- Rising air
- Descending air
- Ocean currents
- Atmospheric winds
- Cloud and heavy rain
- Clear skies

11.1 The ocean–atmosphere interrelationship across the Pacific Ocean under normal conditions

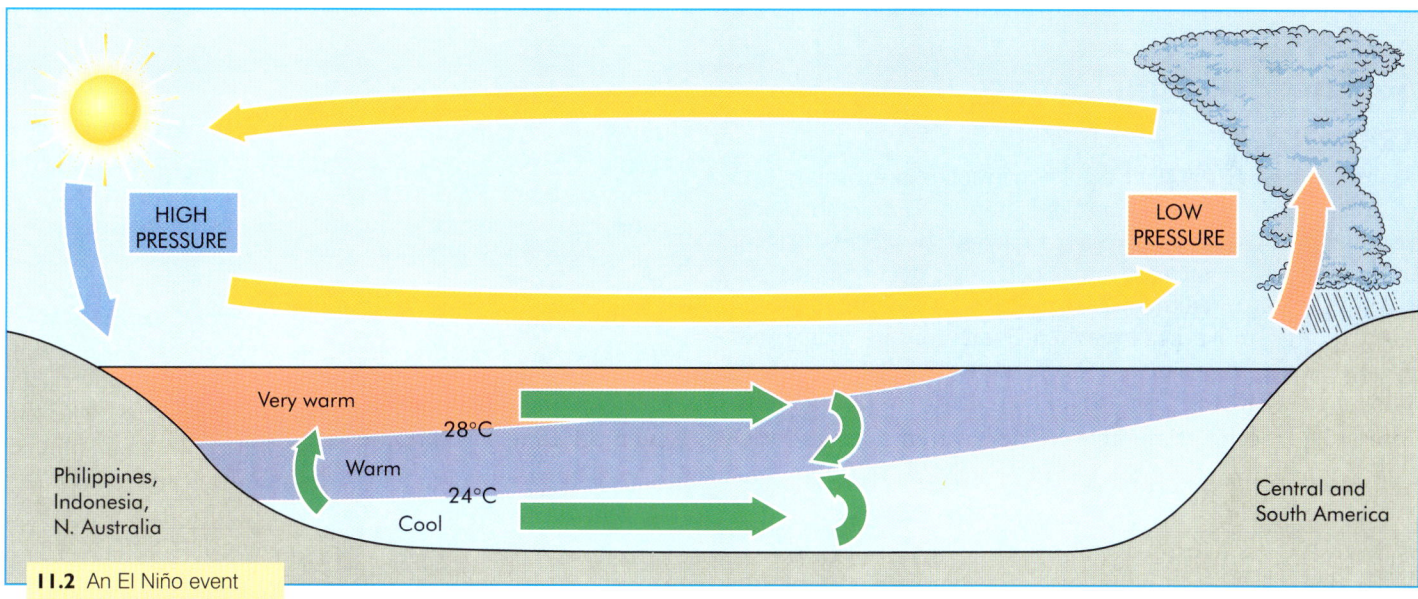

LOW PRESSURE — Philippines, Indonesia, N. Australia
HIGH PRESSURE — Central and South America
Very warm 28°C, Warm 24°C, Cool

11.2 An El Niño event

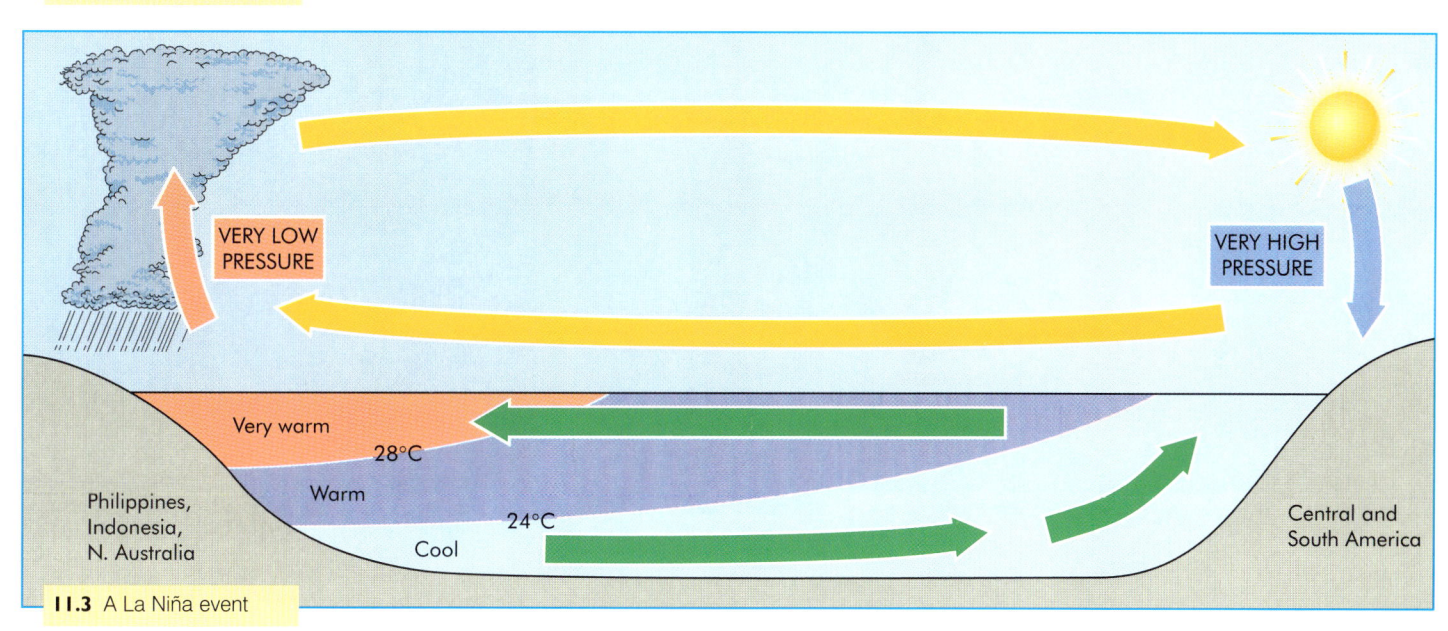

HIGH PRESSURE — Philippines, Indonesia, N. Australia
LOW PRESSURE — Central and South America
Very warm 28°C, Warm 24°C, Cool

11.3 A La Niña event

VERY LOW PRESSURE — Philippines, Indonesia, N. Australia
VERY HIGH PRESSURE — Central and South America
Very warm 28°C, Warm 24°C, Cool

11.4 Extent of the smoke haze in October 1997 and April 1998

South-east Asia – smog

1997–98

From September 1997 to June 1998, much of South-east Asia was blanketed by a thick smoke haze which, in reality, was smog. The so-called haze was caused by thousands of uncontrolled forest fires, most of which occurred on the large Indonesian islands of Borneo and Sumatra (**11.4**). At its peak, the smoke haze reached Thailand, the Philippines and northern Australia, covering an area the size of western Europe and causing visibility to be reduced to under 50 m.

Effects of the smog

Human The air pollution index in Sarawak (**11.4**) reached 852 and on Riau (between Sumatra and Singapore) 978, when a figure of 100 is regarded as unhealthy, and over 300 is considered to be hazardous for human health. This caused great concern for children and high-risk groups already suffering from respiratory (asthma and bronchitis) or cardiovascular (heart) diseases. Schools on Sumatra and in Sarawak were closed and children in the Malaysian capital of Kuala Lumpur were given smog masks which they had to wear each time they went out-of-doors (**11.5**). Little concern was expressed, however, about the fires' effect on the millions of Indonesian people who live in and around the forests.

11.5 Schoolchildren wearing smog masks in Kuala Lumpur

11.6 An orang-utan

Economic Airports throughout the region were closed, logging operations were suspended and farm crops destroyed. An airline crash in Sumatra and a ship collision in the Strait of Malacca were both attributed to the smog. Photographs and reports of smoggy cities caused a drop in the number of tourists and business people visiting the region.

Environmental It was later estimated that 90 per cent of the canopy trees were lost in Sumatra and Borneo, and 10 million ha of forest had been burnt. Regeneration of the forest was predicted to be slow, due to a degradation of the soil, and future fires more likely as the new growth was highly combustible. The fires destroyed numerous wildlife habitats, including those for such endangered species as the orang-utan (**11.6**), the proboscis monkey, the Sumatran rhinoceros and the Sumatran tiger. Carbon dioxide, released by the burning trees, added to global warming.

Causes of the smog

Many rural-dwelling Indonesians, accustomed to living in a hot, wet climate and where dry spells are short-lived, still use methods involving fire in their traditional farming. Fire has long been used as a quick and cheap method of land clearance by farmers (**11.7**) and, more recently, by plantation and forestry-concession owners. In 1997 the monsoon rains failed and the resultant drought was blamed, by scientists, on the El Niño event of that year (page 76). It was this long, dry season (it lasted nearly a year) that encouraged the fires and allowed them to burn out of control. At one stage, 280 separate fires were seen on a flight over Borneo. Although lightning can cause fires, those in Indonesia were caused by people:

- local people clearing land for subsistence farming
- plantation companies converting large areas of forest for rubber and oil palm production
- logging companies, many operating illegally, degrading the natural forest
- ineffectual government action in failing to enforce their own laws forbidding farmers and plantation owners from clearing land during dry seasons.

11.7 A subsistence farmer in Kalimantan

Although the blame for most of the fires was placed upon the many small farmers, satellite photos showed that 80 per cent of the fires were caused by large companies, many of whom had close connections with the then Indonesian President.

Once the fires raged out of control, there was little that a developing country as poor as Indonesia could do. The remoteness of the fires and the lack of resources, organisation and expertise combined to make fire-control impossible. It was only the end of the El Niño event in mid-1998 and the return of the monsoon rains that finally extinguished the fires.

1999

Meteorologists predicted that, with a La Niña event replacing El Niño, 1999 would be wetter than normal and that dry weather was highly unlikely (page 76)). However, perhaps through complacency, or maybe just ignorance or economic pressure, by late July the fires had again begun to spread. Figure **11.8** describes the situation in early August.

A state of emergency has been declared in parts of Indonesia after the return of the deadly smog, caused by forest fires, that disrupted transport, killed wildlife and choked people across South-east Asia two years ago. Local authorities on Riau [**11.4**] have advised people to stay indoors after visibility was reduced to 100 m. Warnings have also been issued to drivers, airlines and to shipping in the Strait of Malacca, one of the world's busiest and most strategically important waterways. Across the strait, the air pollution index was showing levels dangerous to health in Singapore and Malaysia. Neighbouring countries were highly critical of Indonesia's failure to enforce their recommended 'zero-burning' policy.

11.8 1999 – the return of the fires

Global warming – is there a link with ice melt?

Global warming is believed to be responsible for the melting of ice sheets and glaciers. Is there, however, such a simple relationship?

Ice sheets, ice shelves and sea ice

Global warming is said to affect sea-levels by two processes:
1. As sea temperatures rise, the upper layers of the oceans will expand (thermal expansion).
2. As ice sheets in Antarctica and Greenland and glaciers in more temperate latitudes melt, the volume of water in the oceans will increase.

Antarctica is a huge area of land-ice, known as an ice sheet, that extends in places to form ice shelves. Ice shelves, which are floating extensions of the ice sheet, gain new ice from glaciers draining down from the ice sheet, and lose ice as icebergs calving (breaking off) from their ocean edges. Scientists have noted that, since the 1940s, temperatures in Antarctica have risen by 2.5°C – faster than anywhere else in the world. This rapid warming appears to have caused the retreat of several ice shelves (e.g. Larsen A), culminating in 1998 with the break-up of the Larsen B ice shelf (**11.9**). Some environmental groups claim that, unless global warming is reduced immediately, many of Antarctica's ice shelves will melt within decades. However, both the US Geological Survey and the British Antarctic Survey say that there is little evidence of waning ice sheets nor a significant rise in sea-level. (Note, on **11.10**, how Larsen B is located much further from the South Pole than other Antarctic ice shelves.) The two Survey teams claim that whereas melting ice shelves do not affect sea-level (floating ice displaces the equivalent amount of water), the potential sea-level rise, should the whole ice sheet melt, would be 73 m.

75 km² of ice shelf breaks free in Antarctic

Satellite images reveal that a section, 40 km long and 5 km wide, of the Larsen B ice shelf, has broken away from the Antarctic peninsula, confirming an earlier warning by British experts that it was under threat.

The loss of the ice shelf was monitored by scientists analysing images obtained by the polar-orbiting satellite operated by America's National Oceanic and Atmospheric Administration. Images taken in February and March were compared by the University of Colorado at the Boulder-based National Snow and Ice Data Center.

'The Feb 26 image shows that much of the ice was already gone,' says Ted Scambos, research associate at the university's Co-operative Institute for Research in Environmental Sciences.

'The March 23 image made it crystal clear that a significant portion of the shelf had broken off.'

'The warning trend appears to be related to a reduction in sea ice. The question now is what is causing the reduction. At this point we do not have enough evidence to find a smoking gun.'

Newcastle Journal 18.4.98 and Sunday Times 19.4.98

11.9 Break-up of the Larsen B ice shelf

Arctic ice is mainly located over Greenland and around the North Pole. Parts of the Greenland ice sheet have been thinning by more than one metre a year since 1994. Should it melt completely, it could add 7 m to sea-level. The North Pole is covered in sea-ice. Earlier research by James McCarthy, an oceanographer, showed that the average summer thickness of ice at the Pole was 3 m. In August 2000, McCarthy was able to sail directly to the North Pole where he discovered a hole in the ice over 1 km wide (possibly the first time it had not been frozen in 55 million years). Estimates suggest that the area covered by sea-ice is decreasing by 4 per cent of its area annually. In September 2000, for the first time ever, a ship that was not an ice-breaker managed to sail through the North-West Passage – that is, around northern Canada.

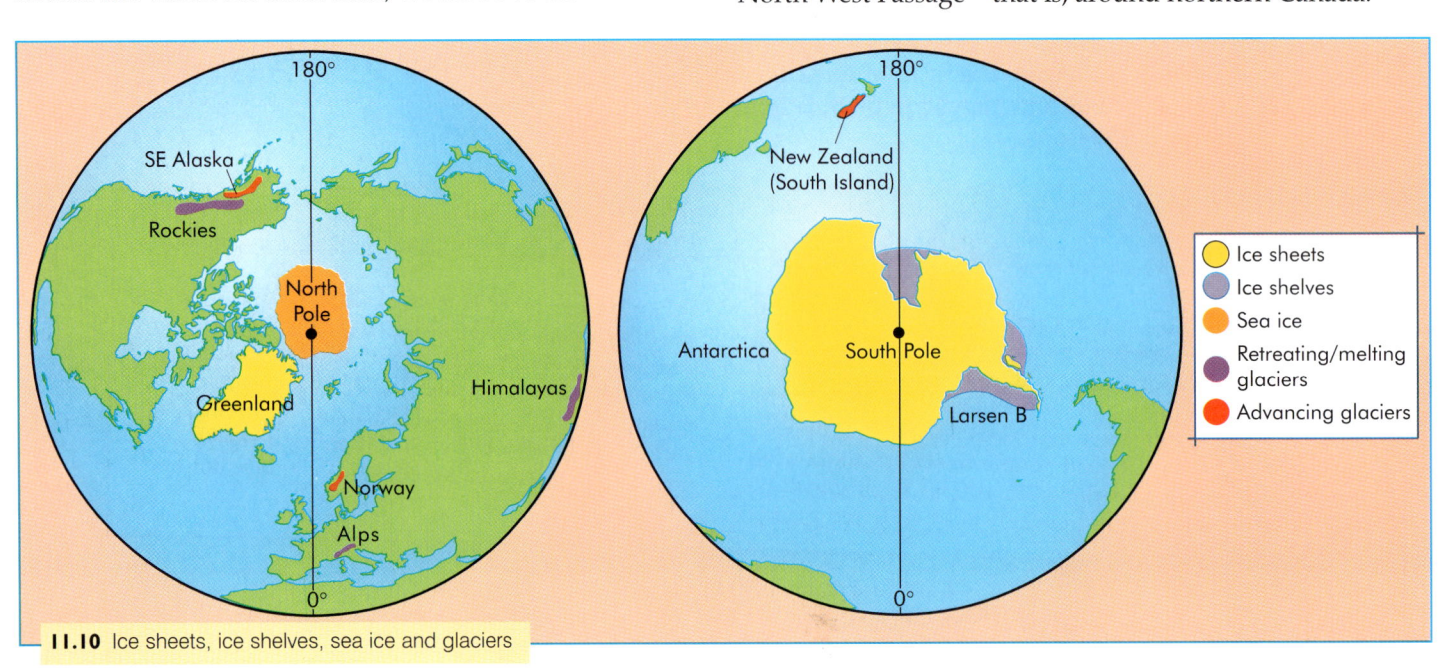

11.10 Ice sheets, ice shelves, sea ice and glaciers

11.11 Franz Josef glacier, New Zealand

11.12 Changing positions of the Franz Josef glacier

Glaciers

Scientists are also concerned that global warming will cause ice and snow stored in glaciers to melt. Indeed, glaciers world-wide are now smaller than at any time in the past 5000 years. Those in the Himalayas, which contain most ice and snow outside the polar ice sheets, are reported to be melting at an alarming rate. Listed as a contributory cause of the 1998 floods in Bangladesh (page 73), one UN study claims that they may all have vanished by 2035. There is evidence that glaciers are retreating in the Canadian Rockies. The Athabasca Glacier, now only 6 km in length (it was 1 km longer in 1960), is a remnant of an ice sheet that once covered 325 km^2.

However, there is also evidence that some glaciers are advancing in three widely spaced parts of the world:

1 In Norway, glaciers leading from the Svartisen and Jostedalsbreen ice caps (an ice cap is a smaller version of an ice sheet) are advancing by more than 0.25 km a year.
2 Glacier Bay, in south-east Alaska, did not exist as a bay when it was 'discovered' in 1794 as it was totally filled by a large glacier (the Grand Pacific Glacier) and its tributaries. By 1925, the glaciers had retreated 100 km inland with a maximum retreat of 1.75 km per year between 1960 and 1980. The glacier then remained more or less stationary until 1990 since when, despite global warming, it has advanced by 0.3 km per year.
3 Franz Josef is the largest of 140 glaciers located in the Westland and Mount Cook National Parks on the South Island of New Zealand. The glacier is channelled down a narrow valley with a steep gradient (**11.11**). Following its most recent maximum advance in 1750, the glacier had retreated by 2 km by 1850, remained almost stationary until the 1930s, and then retreated at an accelerating rate – presumed to be due to the increase in global warming – a further 3 km until 1985. It then suddenly began to re-advance and within 15 years it had extended 2 km back down its valley (**11.12**).

It is the shape and gradient of the valley that makes the Franz Josef highly sensitive to climatic change – though to snowfall rather than to temperature. Whereas snow falling at the head of the Athabasca Glacier takes 150 years to reach the snout, it only takes 5 years on the Franz Josef. Since 1985 there has been an increase in both cloud cover and snowfall in the Mt Cook region and it is this that has presumably caused the glacier to advance. The increase may be due to a rise in temperature (global warming) which allows the air to hold more moisture (increased evaporation) and, when forced to rise over high mountains (as it has to in each of the three locations), increases precipitation (snowfall).

Conclusions

So is global warming causing ice sheets to melt and glaciers to retreat? As in other aspects of geography it is difficult, and at times dangerous, to make a broad generalisation. For example:

- Ice sheets and glaciers are much smaller than they were 5000 years ago, yet global warming is only believed to have begun less than 150 years ago. What caused the ice to melt before global warming?
- Global warming does seem to be causing ice shelves in Antarctica to break up, sea-ice at the North Pole to melt and glaciers in the Himalayas, Alps and Canadian Rockies to retreat.
- Glaciers in Norway, south-east Alaska and New Zealand appear to be advancing.
- There can be differing rates of advance and retreat between neighbouring glaciers.

12 Environmental concerns

UK – brownfield and greenfield sites

Britain is short of houses. Estimates in 1995 suggested that 4.4 million new homes would be needed by 2016. This figure was later revised upwards in 1998 to 5.0 million, and downwards in mid-1999 to 4.1 million. Of these, 1 million had already been built by mid-2000. Assuming the latest estimate to be the most accurate, the question then is, 'Where are these new houses to be built?' In 1998 the government announced that 50 per cent would be built on 'brownfield sites', i.e. on land within existing urban areas, and 50 per cent on 'greenfield sites', i.e. in the countryside. After a major public outcry to 'save the countryside', the government revised the figures to 60 per cent on brownfield sites and 40 per cent on greenfield sites. However, while there are sufficient brownfield sites across the country as a whole, the National Land Use Database shows a mismatch between:

- where pressure for new homes is greatest, i.e. the South East of England
- where most brownfield sites are available, i.e. the Midlands and the North.

Figure **12.1** lists some of the arguments as to why some groups of people would prefer most of the new developments to be on brownfield sites and why others favour greenfield sites.

Why build on brownfield sites?

Groups such as the Council for the Protection of Rural England (CPRE) and Friends of the Earth argue that:

- there are already three-quarters of a million unoccupied houses in cities that could be upgraded (**12.2**)
- a further 1.3 million could be created by either subdividing large houses or using empty space above shops and offices
- according to the database, 1.3 million homes could be built on vacant and derelict land and another 0.3 million by re-using old industrial and commercial premises (**12.3**).
- urban living reduces the need to use the car and maintains services, especially retailing, in city centres.

The government assumes that 80 per cent of the new demand for houses will come from single-parent families who prefer, or need, to live in cities.

Why build on greenfield sites?

Developers claim that:

- most British people want to own their own home, complete with garden, set in a rural, or semi-rural location (unlike most people on the continent who prefer to rent an apartment)
- people are healthier and generally have a better quality of life in rural areas
- at present, for every three people moving into cities (almost 160 000 a year), five move out into the countryside (250 000 a year) – a net loss to urban areas of 90 000 a year
- greenfield sites are cheaper to build on than brownfield sites as they are likely to have lower land values and are less likely to be in need of clearing-up operations (especially if the proposed development is on a former industrial site)
- only 11 per cent of Britain is urbanised, and even if all the new proposed housing development took place on brownfield sites, 87.5 per cent of the country would still be rural.

12.1 Why build on brownfield and greenfield sites?

MORE than 2600 properties are empty in Newcastle's West End at a time when plans are on the table to build 2500 houses in green belt land on the fringe of the city.

In Scotswood alone, there are 31 vacant or under-used sites – mainly house clearance areas – amounting to more than 12 ha.

And since 1981, the city has demolished around 2000 council homes in the West End.

The figures are revealed in a draft report on housing development and land supply in Newcastle to the year 2002.

Meanwhile, the city council is working on a masterplan to guide developers in the 485 ha Northern Development Area bounded by Brunton Park, Gosforth, Fawdon, Kingston Park, Hazlerigg and Red House Farm. Their plans have yet to go before councillors for a decision.

Brian Ham, city director of enterprise, environment and culture, said that even with the development of the greenfield NDA, the city was still confident of meeting the government's target of 60% of homes being built on brownfield, or used, sites. He said that over the next 10 years the city had a target of ensuring that two brownfield homes were built for every one greenfield.

Newcastle Journal, 14 October 1998

12.2 Vacant brownfield sites and proposed greenfield development in Newcastle upon Tyne

12.3 A brownfield site

New housing in South East England

The demand for new housing is greatest in the South East of England where large areas of greenfield sites and land in green belts are under threat (**12.4**). In 1999, the CPRE claimed:

'The capacity of the South East's countryside to accommodate extra housing development is already at a bursting point and increased building rates will have a devastating impact on the environment. The South East faces a nightmare of sprawl and congestion. Building over one million houses will shatter the green belt (12.5), intrude on land protected for its landscape or wildlife value, and lose land at present used for farming and recreation. The government needs, instead, to promote a shift in development pressures towards the renaissance of our major cities and the regions in decline.'

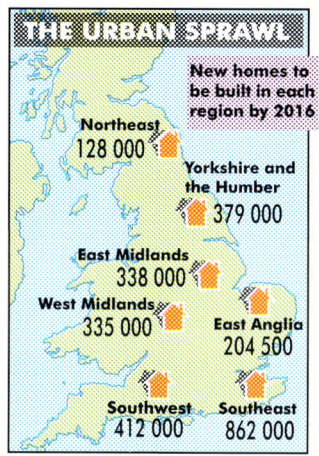

THE URBAN SPRAWL

New homes to be built in each region by 2016

- Northeast 128 000
- Yorkshire and the Humber 379 000
- East Midlands 338 000
- West Midlands 335 000
- East Anglia 204 500
- Southwest 412 000
- Southeast 862 000

THOUSANDS of hectares of greenfield sites are to be concreted to make way for 20 new towns and dozens of housing estates under plans being drawn up by local authorities.

The plans, which fly in the face of government pledges to save the countryside, will hit the south-east of England particularly hard.

Earlier this year John Prescott, the deputy prime minister who has responsibility for the environment, said no more than 40% of the 5 million new homes needed in Britain by 2016 should be built on greenfield sites, with the rest being built on derelict land (i.e. 2 million in total).

Developers have already proposed a new town outside Cambridge – codenamed C2 – which would provide homes for at least 50 000 people. There have also been proposals for two settlements in Devon, a 10 000-home development between Ripon and Thirsk in North Yorkshire, a new town in Worcestershire and a new town with 7000 homes in Hampshire.

'These plans are a disaster for the countryside,' said Tony Burton, of the Council for the Protection of Rural England. 'We don't think there is a need to allocate any more greenfield sites for development. It would undermine the urban renewal which is meant to be the strategy of this government.'

12.4 The urban sprawl

Sunday Times, 5 November 1998

Green Belt homes plan goes ahead

ENVIRONMENTALISTS reacted angrily last night after a council decided to press ahead with plans to build thousands of homes on green belt farmland in Hertfordshire.

Earlier this month thousands of people turned out for a 5 km march and rally through Langley Valley, on the outskirts of Stevenage, which has been earmarked for new homes.

But despite objections, Hertfordshire County Council agreed yesterday to adopt the plan to build 3600 homes on the controversial land. Another 1000 houses will be built on a green belt site in Hemel Hempstead and hundreds of others on smaller areas by the Government's deadline of 2011.

The council said building new homes on the two sites was unavoidable because urban building was reaching saturation point.

12.5 Pressure on the green belt *Daily Telegraph, 1 May 1998*

The CPRE also claim that:
- an area of rural land larger than Greater London has been urbanised in the South East since 1945
- the area of urban derelict land in the South East outside London is rising (it grew by 45 per cent between 1988 and 1993)
- traffic levels on rural lanes in the South East are forecast to more than double by 2030 should there be no changes in policy
- almost two-thirds of South East England is now disturbed by the impact of development and fewer places remain as 'tranquil zones' (**12.6**).

The CPRE defines as a 'tranquil zone':

'...anywhere that lies at least 4 km from a large power station; 3 km from a major motorway, major industrial area or large city; 2 km from other motorways, trunk roads or smaller towns; 1 km from busy local roads carrying more than 10 000 vehicles per day or the busiest main-line railways. It should also lie beyond the interference of civil and military aircraft.'

The rate at which such zones are being eaten away is shown on **12.6**.

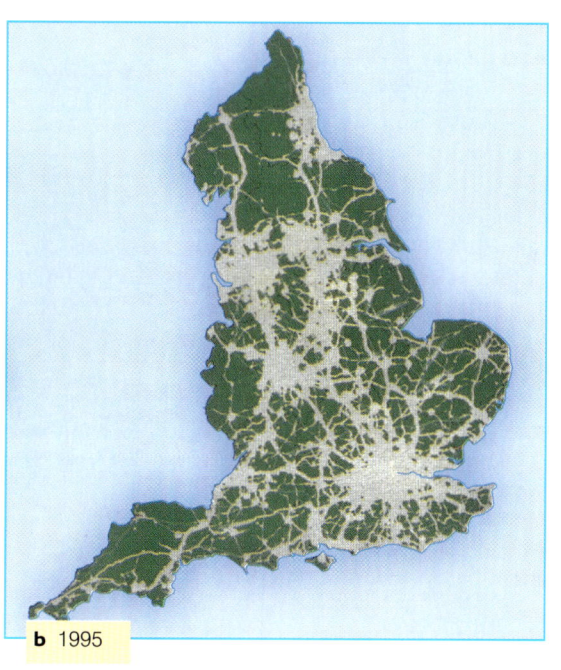

12.6 Decrease of the tranquil zone of England

a 1965

b 1995

Livigno – tourist pressure in the Italian Alps

Before tourism

Livigno, even in the 1960s, was a small, isolated farming village in northern Italy whose inhabitants struggled to earn a living. The type of farming found here – the seasonal movement of animals – was called transhumance. In Livigno, cattle were taken uphill during the short summers to graze on the alpine pastures, and then brought down to the valley floors where they were kept in barns during the long winters. The village lacked electricity (people relied upon candles and oil-lamps) and water had to be obtained from wells. The two roads out of the village were blocked, often from November to March, by snow. The only access to the outside world was across the border into Switzerland – a return journey, on horseback, of 16 hours.

The Swiss then built a hydro-electric power station in the valley above Livigno at a site within Switzerland. As compensation, the Swiss constructed a main road to link Livigno with Switzerland. In one place this road has to pass through a tunnel, and elsewhere it has to be protected by snowsheds from avalanches (pages 62 and 63). The new road not only linked Livigno with Switzerland, it also linked tourists with Livigno. In one generation, the farming village was transformed into a major winter ski resort (**12.7**).

Advantages for winter sports

- Livigno, situated at an altitude of 2400 m, is surrounded by mountains rising to 3000 m. This means that temperatures remain low and snowfalls can be heavy from as early as September until the end of April. This results in an extended winter sports season.
- The floor of the glaciated valley is both flat and, compared with other alpine areas, wide (**12.8**). This allows plenty of space for constructing hotels, flats and restaurants.
- The valley sides are – also compared with other alpine skiing areas – relatively gentle. This makes Livigno an ideal location for novice skiers and families.
- Livigno is cheaper than ski resorts in Austria, France and Switzerland.

12.7 The centre of Livigno

Livigno today

The landscape and the community's way of life have both changed considerably in the last 30 years.
- The settlement now has electricity together with improved water supplies and sewerage.
- On both sides of the valley there is a network of ski-lifts and ski-runs (**12.9**).
- The village has grown into a small town with, at peak periods, up to 13 000 visitors, who outnumber local people by more than 4 to 1.
- Farmhouses and family homes are swamped by the buildings that go with a tourist boom – hotels, chalets, souvenir shops, restaurants, bars and clubs.

12.8 The situation of Livigno

12.9 Ski-lifts above Livigno

12.10 Specialist ski equipment

- The development of the resort has led to the 'multiplier effect', i.e. the attraction of other types of economic activity, many of which are labour intensive, that have created even more jobs and wealth (page 37). These include providing accommodation, shops for specialist winter clothing (**12.10**), and places to eat, drink and for evening entertainment.
- There are better-paid jobs (one former farmer and his wife now have their own hotel, music store and souvenir shop – **12.11**) and more jobs (less need for younger villagers to leave Livigno to seek work) for local people.

- There is an increase in people coming from beyond Livigno seeking work. These include people:
  – who have migrated from other parts of Italy (page 34) where jobs are in short supply, e.g. a chef from Sicily (**12.12**) who met his future wife who is from Sardinia
  – who come seeking part-time or seasonal work, e.g. tour reps, ski-instructors, hotel cleaners and bar-tenders.

Although tourism has brought many benefits to Livigno, it has also, as in other alpine ski resorts, had an adverse effect upon both the local community and the local environment (**12.13**).

12.11 A souvenir shop

12.12 Chef in a local restaurant

Community impact	Environmental impact
■ The village is now totally reliant upon tourism. ■ Farmers have lost their jobs. ■ House prices have risen and become too expensive for many local people. ■ There is seasonal unemployment because most jobs are limited to the winter skiing season. ■ The traditional way of life has changed due to an increase in traffic and people.	■ Visual eye-sores of ski-lifts (**12.9**) and buildings extending up the hillside. ■ The land has been deforested for new and longer ski-runs and for better access roads. This increases the risk of soil erosion and avalanches (page 62). ■ Skiing can destroy the fragile arctic/alpine ecosystem. ■ There is congestion on local roads and parking problems for cars, motor-homes and buses. ■ The huge increase in traffic is blamed for adding to the acid rain that is killing local vegetation.

12.13 Impact of tourism on the local community and environment

Northern India – quarrying and the environment

The limestone that is quarried in the Himalayas is either crushed and added to molten steel for use in the Indian car industry, or is used for road building, concrete or whitewash. As India's economy continues to grow, there is an increasing conflict between development and the environment. The extraction of rocks and minerals is necessary to provide manufacturing industry with raw materials and to provide people with jobs, but mining and quarrying can be very damaging to the environment and fragile ecosystems (**12.14**).

Dehra Dun is the main town in the Dun Valley. The town, situated in the foothills of the Himalayas some 200 km north and east of Delhi, has a population of 400 000 and is growing fast. The town is the location for some of India's most prestigious boarding schools and is known for its sulphur springs. Until the 1960s, the rich soil had allowed farmers to produce high-quality basmati rice, and the lush hill forest surrounding the town had been used sustainably by local people. That was to change when, during the 1960s, many quarries were opened up in the valley to the north of the town. For 25 years these quarries were allowed to operate without any regard for either the inhabitants or the environment of the valley.

How did quarrying affect the environment?

- Blasting the rock (**12.15**) created noise and dust (air pollution). It also caused rocks to fall onto the village of Sahastradhara, situated below the quarries, destroying some of the buildings and killing cattle and buffalo. The explosions also caused buildings to vibrate.
- Quarry workers used to roll the rubble downhill as this was a quick, easy and cheap method of transport. They were unconcerned at the damage that the boulders did to trees growing on the hillsides or to houses in the village.
- Before the quarries, the area was prosperous with green forests (**12.16a**) and plenty of fuelwood that could be used for heating and cooking. Debris from the quarries destroyed many trees and reduced the supply of fuelwood (**12.16b**).
- As new quarries developed, more and more trees on the hillsides were removed. Deforestation in an area with a monsoon climate meant that, when the heavy summer rains came, there was severe soil erosion on the steep hillsides. The rain also caused fertile fields to be covered in debris (**12.17**) and created landslides where the unstable quarry waste had been dumped.
- Material carried downhill was likely to end up in rivers. The debris not only polluted water supplies, it also blocked the river with boulders and silt. Before quarrying, one bridge had an arch 20 m in height. After quarrying, it was only 3 m above the debris (**12.18**).

12.14 Quarrying limestone

12.15 Blasting limestone

12.16 The green forests

a Before quarrying began

b After quarrying

12.17 Limestone debris covering the fields

12.18 River channel choked by debris

- In the 1950s, water was provided all the year round for places like Sahastradhara and Dehra Dun by 'a thousand springs' where rivers, having flowed underground through the limestone, appeared on the surface. Many of these springs became blocked by debris from the quarries, and the increase in surface runoff following deforestation resulted in the water table falling by 5 m in seven years. This meant that:
  a Dehra Dun, with its growing population, often only had four hours of water a day
  b farmers near Sahastradhara had insufficient water for irrigation and, instead of being able to grow sufficient to feed their families, they could only provide enough food for 4 or 5 months.
  c fewer tourists visited the partly dried-out sulphur springs.
- The trucks and lorries, many of them old and badly maintained, that transported the limestone down the steep, narrow roads caused the road surface to break up, released poisonous fumes and created dust.
- The kilns that processed the limestone added to the air pollution (**12.19**).

Local protests against the quarries

In the 1980s, local people grouped together to form the 'Friends of the Dun'. The group, mainly professional, business and retired people (i.e. people who had wealth and influence) collected many signatures and submitted a petition to the Supreme Court. In 1988 the Court ordered all quarries, with one exception, to be closed down. Schoolchildren and local people began to replant trees and by 1995, although farmers still found much of their land unusable, the green forests were returning.

Should the one quarry remain open?

The Supreme Court allowed one quarry to operate until its lease runs out. This was because the quarry:
- provides hundreds of jobs, even if they are poorly paid, for local people
- is attempting conservation techniques by
  a working on a series of flat terraces (**12.20**) so that rubble does not roll down the hillside and into rivers, in order to avoid a further loss of vegetation and water supply
  b re-profiling and replanting areas where quarrying has finished.

The argument now appears to be between the wealthy conservation group, who want to protect and restore the Dun Valley, and the poorer workers who, without the quarry and with no alternative jobs available, would have no income.

12.19 Pollution from the limestone kilns

12.20 Present-day quarry with 'steps'

87

Northern Shaanxi – soil conservation in China

Soil erosion

Northern Shaanxi is located on the southern fringe of the Mu Us desert and on the loess plateau (see **1.6**). Loess is a fine-grained, yellow-coloured material (**6.18**) that was blown to this part of China by Arctic winds during and following the last ice age. In parts of the basin of the Huang He (or the 'Yellow River', referring to the colour given to it by the loess that it transports – page 46), the deposited material has a depth of over 200 m. Although loess is very fertile, being light and porous, it is easily eroded by water and the wind (**6.19**).

According to historical records, Shaanxi was once a place of fertile soil with plenty of water and lush grass. Due to a series of internal wars and excessive land reclamation schemes, the province, as well as the rest of the loess plateau, suffered increasingly from serious soil erosion and the destruction of the ecological environment (**12.21** and **12.22**). This was made worse by the removal – mainly under the direction of Chairman Mao – of most of the remaining grass and trees to allow cereal farming. According to *China Pictorial Publications* (1999):

> 'Further soil erosion led to serious desertification (creating sand dunes that buried farmland and villages) and frequent droughts, floods and wind storms, all of which hindered the development of the local economy. Agriculture fell into a vicious circle: people, because of their poverty, reclaimed more land but the more land they reclaimed (because it was marginal for farming) the poorer they became due to an increase in the rate and scale of soil erosion.'

Soil conservation

Since the early 1980s, the central government has encouraged a comprehensive programme for erosion control on the loess plateau. The two main aims have been:

1 To control and stabilise drifting sand in northern Shaanxi. This has been achieved by building a shelter-forest network and planting trees in the desert margins (**12.23**). In one district alone, trees have been planted on 1 million ha, and land covered by trees has risen from 1.8 per cent in 1950 to 42.9 per cent in 1999 (**12.24**). This has encouraged the return of birds and wildlife, reduced the number of sandstorms and restricted the amount of soil washed into the rivers. Trees have also been planted alongside roads to reduce the power of the wind (**12.25**).

12.21 Gullies caused by erosion of the loess

12.22 Soil-eroded hillsides (background) and stone-bordered fields

12.23 The shelter-forest network

12.24 Pits dug on mountain slopes for planting trees

2 To improve the quality of the loess soil throughout Shaanxi. This has involved the terracing of hillsides (**12.26**), the development of irrigation schemes (**6.22** and **6.23**) and the construction of check-dams. Check-dams are built across small river valleys to trap any silt-laden water. The silt is allowed to settle, creating new farmland, before the water is allowed to drain away.

Quoting again from *China Pictorial Publications* (1999):
'The countryside is again looking green. Yields have increased considerably, there is a surplus of grain [see **6.24**] and farming is more diversified with the production of cash crops that include tobacco, fruit and vegetables [**6.25**]. Rainfall has increased and droughts are less serious. The average income of farmers has trebled (from 400 to 1220 yuan in less than a decade) and many people who had previously left due to poverty have returned.'

A further programme to combat soil erosion, this time by the Shaanxi provincial government, was reported in the *China Daily* of 11 May 1999 (**12.27**).

12.25 Trees planted beside the road as a windbreak

12.26 Terraces cut in a loess hillside

The new programme, announced in January, aims to conserve water and reduce soil erosion by capping the mountains with pine trees, planting forests around the middle part of the mountains and enclosing terraces with rocks in the valley. The main aims of the programme are to hold back water in the mountains and to enlarge the cultivated area in the valleys. By March, residents had planted 12 380 ha of trees for commercial use and were now busy clearing stones and using them to make terraces along the gentle lower slopes of the valley [**12.22**].

Already, many farmers under the new ecology programme have their own patch of forest on the mountain and have doubled the size of their family plots in the valley. The head of a village involved in the programme claimed that it had been the increase in family income, rather than the programmes themselves, that had been the greatest impetus for people to adopt soil conservation methods.

Adapted from *China Daily*, May 1999

12.27 Latest soil conservation project in Shaanxi

Yunnan – re-afforestation in the Upper Yangtze basin

Despite its size, relatively little of China is covered in forest. This is partly because conditions in the western provinces are either too cold or too dry for forests to grow (pages 6 and 7) and partly because, throughout the country's long history, there has been massive felling of trees in the eastern provinces to meet China's need for forest products. Until recently there has been little attempt to replace the vast area of forest that has been cleared for settlement, industry and agriculture. By 1950, only 8 per cent of the country remained under forest and much of that was to disappear under Chairman Mao's 'Great Leap Forward'. Since the introduction of the responsibility system in 1979 (page 43), 1 million ha of new or regenerated forest has been added each year. By 1998, the area of China under forest had increased to 14 per cent, with the aim of reaching 20 per cent by 2020.

Yunnan

Yunnan, much of which is mountainous and remote, was densely forested until the 1950s and, even today, the tropical rainforests of the extreme south of the province remain largely untouched. Less protected have been the mixed forests of northern Yunnan where in the Upper Yangtze basin both the valley sides of the river and other large areas of land have been cleared (**12.28** and **12.29**). The trees were felled either to smelt copper (in previous centuries) and iron ore (in the 20th century), or to clear land for farming (notice the terraces on **12.28**). These clearances have caused problems for the two large ethnic minority groups, the Naxi (page 15) and the Li, who live in this area. This is because both groups of people rely heavily upon the forest to:

- conserve water and to protect the soil from erosion

and to provide:

- timber for their houses (**12.30**)
- fuelwood for heating and cooking (**12.31**)
- fodder for their animals
- food such as wild vegetables, strawberries, mushrooms and wild herbs, together with some wild animals
- materials for stuffing their bedding (Spanish moss), making baskets (bamboo)
- plants for medicines.

12.29 Effects of felling in northern Yunnan

The rate of deforestation and, as a consequence, soil erosion increased rapidly during the Great Leap Forward of the late 1950s. The extra silt washed into the Upper Yangtze in Yunnan was later to be blamed for the floods of later years in the Middle and Lower Yangtze basins (page 74). Indeed it was after the disastrous floods of 1997, and before those of 1998, that the Chinese government decreed an immediate ban on further tree-felling in the region – a decision that cost as many as 120 000 jobs in Yunnan (timber-felling was a huge industry).

12.28 Deforestation on hillsides where the Upper Yangtze enters the Tiger Leaping Gorge

Huize county is located east of Lijiang. It was subjected to a severe flood in 1985 in which crops were lost and houses destroyed. The provincial government began a programme of forced reafforestation in which they provided the seedlings, fertiliser and expertise while the local farmers had to provide the labour. Although there has not been a flood since, the scheme has not pleased the local people. This is mainly because the farmers were given no option but to grow trees on some of their farmland, and those trees had to be pine (**12.32**). Although pines are cheap to plant and they grow quickly, they are of little economic value to the farmers:

- Despite their rate of growth, it takes several years before the trees are ready to be felled. Then, as their value and use is limited, they are only likely to give a meagre financial return – a return that the farmers have to share with the government.
- The trees were planted on cultivated land. This meant that, as many farmers lost land previously used for crops and animals, they could no longer support their own families.
- As the trees were planted close together, the amount of undergrowth was restricted. This meant that there was no grass for the cattle to graze on and no berries or fruit for people to pick.

Since then several less disruptive schemes have been introduced. For example:

- Farmers, now given the choice as to which trees they prefer to grow, are planting sweet chestnuts (**12.33**); these trees provide chestnuts that can be sold in local markets and wood that is good for burning.
- They are also using high-yielding seeds and polythene irrigation techniques.

The recent attempts to manage China's forests have led to a conflict of interest between two groups of people who have different interests and who live in different parts of the basin. Farmers of the Upper Yangtze are resentful at the loss of their farmland and livelihood, due to re-afforestation. They see this as a benefit only to city dwellers living in the lower basin and who have now had the constant threat of flooding caused by deforestation partly removed. Despite the fears of the Yunnan farmers, China seems determined to push ahead with its tree-planting schemes.

12.30 Wooden houses in Lijiang

12.31 Fuelwood is used for cooking

12.32 Young pine trees

12.33 Fertiliser being applied to a young sweet chestnut tree

The Three Gorges Project – benefits and dangers

The Chinese have talked about building a dam across the Yangtze River since the beginning of the 20th century, but it was not until 1994 that work began on the Three Gorges Project (TGP). TGP is a multipurpose scheme aimed at flood control, power generation and navigation improvement. The site, at Sandouping, is where the Yangtze leaves the third, and last, of its three scenic gorges (**12.34**) and is where the river crosses a band of resistant granite (**12.35**). The building of the dam, which is 185 m high and 1983 m (2 km) wide (**10.13**), the two power stations and the giant ship-locks, is a monumental engineering feat (**8.8**). However, the construction of the project, the scale of which has never been previously attempted, has generated massive controversy mainly due to the likely effects on local people and the unknown effects of interference with the natural functioning of a major river and the surrounding environment (**12.34**). Serious doubts remain as to the TGP's long-term economic, social and ecological costs. Figure **12.36** lists some of the many arguments for and against the project.

Advantages

- The main object of the TGP is to provide flood protection for up to 100 million people living downriver (pages 74 and 75). Large areas downstream of the dam were flooded for several weeks at a time in the 1980s and in 1997 and 1998. The dam is intended to prevent a repeat of the 1998 event when up to 3000 people died, 5.6 million homes were washed away, and 30 million people were made homeless (**10.11**). The dam will also, by creating a large lake behind it, prevent the considerable seasonal variation in the level of flow upstream, often over 8 m a year (**10.12**).
- The second advantage will be the generation of hydro-electricity (page 61) from the two power stations at the dam (**8.8**). Apart from China needing the extra energy if it is to develop its industries and improve its people's standard of living, hydro-electricity is a clean fuel. At present most of China's energy comes from coal – a major cause of global warming and acid rain. By reducing coal consumption by 50 million tonnes a year, the TGP should mean less pollution and less risk to people's health.
- The Yangtze is the main transport route inland from the coast (**12.37** and **12.38**). At present ships of only 1500 tonnes can reach Chongqing because the river flows too fast during the summer flood, and is too low, with exposed rocks, in the dry season. The eventual 600 km lake will allow safe navigation throughout the year for vessels up to 10 000 tonnes. These will pass through the dam by either the ship-lock (**12.39**) or the ship-lift (**8.8**). Tourism should benefit as cruise ships will be able to sail at all times.
- The many new settlements that are being created (**10.16**) will have better housing (with electricity, running water and, in time, sewerage), transport links and services.
- Influenced by the lake, the winter climate should become milder and wetter, allowing local farmers to increase their income by growing citrus fruits.

12.36 Advantages and disadvantages of the Three Gorges Project

12.37 Barges and a cruise-ship on the Yangtze

12.38 Old and new: a sampan and a hydrofoil

12.34 Scenery within the Three Gorges

12.35 The Three Gorges Project

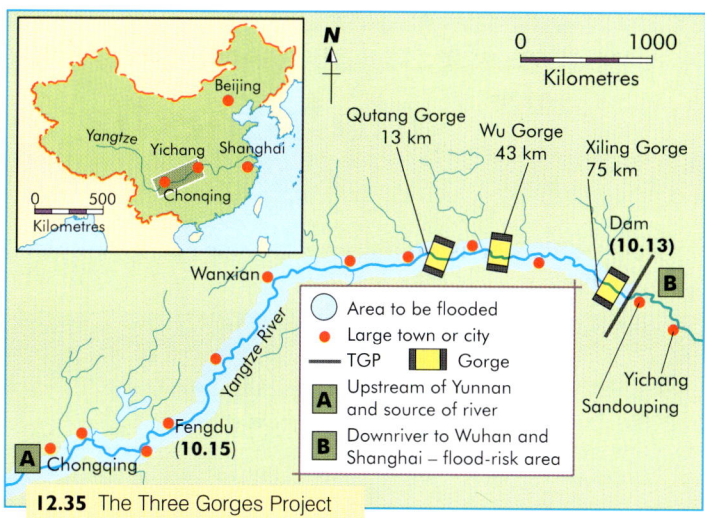

Disadvantages

- The TGP means the relocation of between 1.2 and 1.3 million people whose homes will be inundated as the lake water rises. In total, 4 cities, 8 towns and 356 large villages will be submerged (10.15 and 12.35). People forced to leave their homes are given little choice as to where they can resettle. Although each family is being given compensation towards their removing and rebuilding costs, the amount is insufficient to pay for the modern, but more expensive, houses. As the best sites for settlements have already been used, or will be flooded, many people are being forced (despite original promises to the contrary) to move to more distant provinces. The lake will also flood many temples and sacred places, the best farmland in the valley, and thousands of small factories located alongside the present river (7.6). There are fears that many of the factories, once they have been abandoned and submerged, will release toxic waste, poisoning the waters of the lake.
- The Yangtze transports vast amounts of silt downriver each year. As the dam will trap this sediment, the lake will, in time, silt up. Although the dam has been designed with special sluices to allow sediment to pass downriver, there are fears that:
  a a delta will form at the head of the lake, eventually blocking the port of Chongqing and
  b reduced sediment downriver will damage agriculture in places near the delta where farmers rely on fertile silt to improve their fields.
- At present, sewage from cities alongside the Yangtze, including those being built to rehouse the people being displaced, is allowed to flow downriver and out to sea. Presumably, until treatment works are built, this and other rubbish will also be trapped (12.40).
- There is concern that the dam could break. This might be due to the sheer weight of water, to earthquakes, bad construction, or enemy/terrorist activity.
- There is concern that tourism might be affected if the scenic quality of the Three Gorges is lost, and that endangered species such as the Yangtze sturgeon and the river dolphin will become extinct.
- The cost of the project is likely to exceed US$75 billion – far in excess of the original budget.

12.39 Ship-locks under construction at the dam

12.40 Rubbish and sewage on the Yangtze

Multimedia cross-reference matrix

Chapter	Pages	Title	CD-ROM units	Channel 4 Programmes
1 Physical contrasts in China	4–5	Climatic contrasts	3	Place and People: Changing China Programme 1 *Farming North and South*
	6–7	Climate and physical regions	1, 2, 3, 7, 10	Place and People: Changing China Programme 1 *Farming North and South*
2 Population changes	8–9	World trends	–	–
	10	Italy – changing population structures	–	Place and People: Italy Programme 1 *The Deep South:* The story of now
	11	India – family planning	–	–
	12–13	China – population growth and the one-child policy	4	–
	14–15	China – an ageing population and minority ethnic groups	4, 7, 14	Place and People: Changing China Programme 3 *Forestry, Flooding and Farming*
3 Changing villages	16–17	Thurston – a suburbanised village in the UK	–	Geographical Eye over Britain (1) Programme 4 *The Changing Village:* East Anglia
	18–19	Castleton – a village in a UK National Park	–	–
		Hennock, Rookhope and Longnor – villages in remote areas of the UK	–	–
	20–21	Uti and Ooruttukala – villages in southern India	–	Geographical Eye over Asia Programme 1 *India: Farming and Development*
	22–23	Hua Long – a village in Sichuan, central China	5, 7, 10	Place and People: Changing China Programme 1 *Farming North and South*
4 Urban management	24–25	UK – traffic management	–	–
	26–27	Lille – an integrated traffic system	–	–
	28–29	Jakarta – urban change in Indonesia	–	Geographical Eye over Asia Programme 6 *Urban Development in Jakarta*
	30–31	Kunming – changing residential areas in a Chinese city	6	–
	32–33	Shanghai – rapid urban change in China	6, 8, 9, 12	Place and People: Changing China Programme 5 *Urban Development in Shanghai*
5 Farming and industry in Italy and India	34–35	Sicily – changes in farming in southern Italy	–	Place and People: Italy Programme 4 *The Land*
	36–37	Melfi – changes in industry in southern Italy	–	Place and People: Italy Programme 1 *The Deep South:* The story of now
	38–39	Kerala – changes in farming in southern India	–	Geographical Eye over Asia Programme 1 *India: Farming and Development*
	40–41	Ahmadabad – changes in the textile industry in India	–	Geographical Eye over Asia Programme 3 *India: The Textile Industry*
6 Farming in China	42–43	China – farming types and changes in farming	7	Place and People: Changing China Programme 1 *Farming North and South*
	44–45	Sichuan and northern Yunnan – rice farming	7	Place and People: Changing China Programme 1 *Farming North and South*
	46–47	Shaanxi and Shanxi – wheat, maize and market gardening	1, 2, 7, 13	Place and People: Changing China Programme 1 *Farming North and South*
	48–49	Northern Yunnan – Naxi farming	4, 7	Place and People: Changing China Programme 1 *Farming North and South*

7 Industry in China	50–51	Changes and types of industry	4, 8, 12	–
	52–53	Xizhang – a township and village enterprise (Beibei Shoe Company)	–	Place and People: Changing China Programme 4 *Township Enterprises and Migration*
	54–55	Suzhou – a silk factory	8	–
	56–57	Shenzhen – high-tech industry in a Special Economic Zone (SEZ)	6, 9	Place and People: Changing China Programme 5 *Urban Development in Shanghai*
8 Changes in energy	58–59	UK – wind farms	–	–
	60–61	China – from coal to hydro-electricity	3, 8. 10, 12	Place and People: Changing China Programme 2 *The Three Gorges Dam*
9 Hazards	62–63	Austria – avalanches	–	–
	64–65	Southern Italy – earthquakes	–	–
	66–67	Merapi – a volcano in Indonesia	–	Geographical Eye over Asia Programme 5 *Indonesia: Story of a Volcano*
	68–69	Hong Kong – typhoons	3, 9	Geographical Eye over Asia Programme 4 *Bangladesh: Living with Flooding*
10 River flooding and management	70–71	The rivers Severn and Wye – flood hazard in the UK	–	–
	72–73	Bangladesh – the river flood of 1998	–	Geographical Eye over Asia Programme 4 *Bangladesh: Living with Flooding*
	74–75	The Yangtze (China) – river flooding: natural and human	3, 12, 13	Place and People: Changing China Programme 2 *The Three Gorges Dam* Programme 3 *Forestry, Flooding and Farming*
11 Climatic issues	76–77	El Niño and La Niña – climatic change	–	–
	78–79	South-east Asia – smog	–	–
	80–81	Global warming – is there a link with ice melt?	–	–
12 Environmental concerns	82–83	UK – brownfield and greenfield sites	–	–
	84–85	Livigno – tourist pressure in the Italian Alps	–	Place and People: Italy Programme 3 *Alps under Stress*
	86–87	Northern India – quarrying and the environment	–	Geographical Eye over Asia Programme 2 *Environment and Industry*
	88–89	Northern Shaanxi – soil conservation in China	1, 2, 3, 13	Place and People: Changing China Programme 1 *Farming North and South* Programme 3 *Forestry, Flooding and Farming*
	90–91	Yunnan – re-afforestation in the Upper Yangtze basin	1, 2, 3, 13, 14	Place and People: Changing China Programme 3 *Forestry, Flooding and Farming*
	92–93	The Three Gorges Project – benefits and dangers	1, 3, 8, 9, 11, 12, 13	Place and People: Changing China Programme 2 *The Three Gorges Dam*

The CD–ROM *Images of Change: China* by David Waugh and Chris Rowley is obtainable from:

Geopix Ltd
Crookside
Heads Nook
Brampton
CA8 9AA

e-mail: office@geopix–Ltd.demon.co.uk

Videos of the Channel 4 series *Place and People* and *Geographical Eye* are available from:

4Learning
PO Box 100
Warwick
CV34 6TZ

Telephone: 01926 436444
e-mail: sales@4learning.co.uk
Fax: 01926 436446
Website: www.4learning.co.uk/shop

Index

All **places** are shown in **bold**.

Alps	62–3, 84–5
Austria	62–3
avalanches	62–3
Bangladesh	72–3
brownfield/greenfield sites	82–3
China	
climate	4–7
energy	60–1
ethnic minority groups	14–5, 48–9
farming	42–9
Hong Kong	68–9
Hua Long	22–3
industry	50–7
Kunming	30–1
population	12–15
Pudong	32–3
re-afforestation	88–91
residential areas	28–32
river flooding	74–5
rural settlement	22–3
Shaanxi	46–7, 88–9
Shanghai	32–3
Shanxi	42, 46–7
Shenzhen	56–7
Sichuan	7, 22–3, 42, 44–5
soil erosion/management	88–91
Suzhou	54–5
Three Gorges	61, 74–5, 92–3
township and village enterprises	52–3
transport	32–3, 92
typhoons	68–9
urban settlement	30–3
villages	22–3
Xizhang	52–3
Yangtze	60–1, 74–5, 92–3
Yunnan	7, 15, 42, 44–5, 48–9, 90–1
climate	
change	76–7, 80–1
hazards	68–9, 76–81
earthquakes	64–5
El Niño/La Niña	76–7
energy	
coal	60
hydro-electricity	60–1, 92
wind farms	58–9
environmental issues	70–93
ethnic minority groups	14–15, 48–9
farming	
China	42–9
India	38–9
Italy	34–5
flooding	70–5, 92–3
France	
Lille	26–7
glaciers	80–1
hazards	62–75
ice sheets	80–1
India	
Ahmadabad	40–1
farming	38–9
Himalayas	86–7
industry	40–1
Kerala	20–1, 38–9
population	11
quarrying	86–7
rural settlement	20–1
Indonesia	
Jakarta	28–9
Merapi	66–7
smog	78–9
volcanoes	66–7
industry	
cars	36–7
China	50–7
high-tech	56–7
India	40–1
Italy	36–7
silk	54–5
textiles	40–1, 54–5
township and village enterprises	52–3
Italy	
Alps	84–5
Assisi	65
earthquakes	64–5
farming	34–5
industry	36–7
Livigno	84–5
Melfi	36–7
population	10
Sicily	34–5
tourism	84–5
population	
ageing	9–10, 14–15
China	12–15
ethnic minority groups	15
family planning	11–13
fertility rates	8–12
India	11
Italy	10
life expectancy	9–10, 14
one-child policy	12–13
structures	10–15
world trends	8–9
quarrying	86–7
re-afforestation	88–91
residential areas	28–32
river flooding	70–5, 92–3
rural settlement	16–23
smog	78–9
soil erosion/management	88–91
South-east Asia	78–9
suburbanised villages	16–17
tourism	18, 84–5
transport	24–9, 32–3, 92
typhoons	68–9
UK	
brownfield/greenfield sites	82–3
Castleton	18
energy	58–9
Hennock, Rookhope and Longnor	19
river flooding	70–1
rural settlement	16–19
Severn and Wye	70–1
Thurston	16–17
tourism	18
transport	24–5
villages	16–19
wind farms	58–9
urban problems/development	24–33
villages	16–23
volcanic eruptions	66–7
world	
climatic change	76–7, 80–1